Forgive Yourself

Empower Yourself by Letting Go of the Past and Overcoming Your Feelings of Guilt

Table of Contents

Introduction

Self-forgiveness is a process

Expressing unpleasant feelings directed toward yourself

Developing good feelings directed toward yourself

Accepting responsibility

The 4 Rs Of Self-Forgiveness

Responsibility

Remorse

Restoration

Renewal

Why Is It Hard To Forgive Yourself?

Why Should We Embrace Self-Forgiveness?

Chapter 1: It's Not Your Fault. Stop Dealing With It.

Telltale Signs of Self-Blame

Toxic self-criticism

Black-and-white thinking

Chronic self-doubt

Unfulfilling relationships

Self-harm and poor self-care

The Causes of Self-Blame

Unresolved Trauma

Depression

Anxiety

Obsessive-Compulsive Disorder(OCD)

The Three Strategies for Letting Go of Unhealthy Guilt

Be realistic about what is controllable

Use Affirmations

Challenge Perfectionism

Be assertive to those who instill guilt for no reason

Chapter 2: Maybe It Was Your Fault. That's okay.

Why can't you stop thinking, 'It's All My Fault?

You get to feel sorry for yourself

You gain attention

You maintain control

It gives you power

You can avoid changing

You don't have to be vulnerable

The price of always taking the blame

Even Things That Seem Like Your Fault Probably Aren't

Financial Crisis

Health Crisis

Boredom and Emptiness

Confusion

Friendship Problems

Haunting Past

Safety and Security

Failure

Grief

The Bottom Line

Twelve Things You Must Stop Blaming Yourself For

Your emotions

The way you handle those emotions

Another person's rejection

Little failures and significant failures

Someone else's circumstances

Your needs

Your guilty pleasures

Being terrible at something

Putting yourself first before everyone and everything else

Trusting somebody, you shouldn't have

A terminated relationship

Whatever happened in the past

Three Strategies For Finding The Real Causes Of Problems That Seem To Come From You

Analyze your problem

Eliminate facts from fiction

Ask for others' input.

Chapter 3: So It Was Your Fault? You're Still a Good Person

Does feeling guilty for causing a problem prove that you are good?

Guilt Vs. Empathy

Do Intentions Matter? If Yours Are Good, Does It Mean Your Behavior Is Excusable?

Examples of good intentions gone bad

Find out what is wrong with your behavior.

Picture the Outcome You Desire

The solution lies in the gap.

Three Strategies for Forgiving Yourself When You Know You're in The Wrong

Disconnect Your Identity From Your Mistakes

Record your thoughts and feelings

Ask For Forgiveness

Chapter 4: Why It Is Moral to Forgive Yourself

Why It Is Compassionate to Forgive Yourself

Why It Is Fair to Forgive Yourself

Why It Is Empowering to Forgive Yourself

Why It Is Loving to Forgive Yourself

Why The World Wants You to Forgive Yourself

Chapter 5: Why It Is Socially Responsible to Forgive Yourself

Society Benefits When You Forgive Yourself

Self-forgiveness nurtures relationships

Forgiveness Can Transform General Attitudes

Self-forgiveness encourages helping needy society members.

Friends and Family Benefit When You Forgive Yourself

The Future Becomes Better When You Forgive Yourself

Chapter 6: How Society Conditions You to Feel Guilt You Do Not Deserve

How Society Conditions Undeserved Blame

Societal Expectations

Culture

Religion

Social pressure

Tons of Oppressive Institutions Propel Shame

We Can't Stop Society, But We Can Protect Ourselves

Avoid Being Around The Perpetrators

Avoid negative news on tv, in newspapers, or on social media

Stay Positive

Label your thoughts

Notice when you're getting into the mean, negative cycle

Pause

Taming Your Ego

Bow into our human condition

Get introspective

Ask for feedback

Stay open to critique.

Enlist a therapist

Chapter 7: Proven Strategies for Overcoming Feelings of Guilt Alone

Sometimes, We Must Overcome Guilt by Ourselves

Name your guilt

Explore the source of your guilt

Learn from the past

Replace Negative Self-Talk With Compassion For Yourself

Create an Action Plan to Overcome Guilt

Define your problem

Write a solution for each situation.

Implement your Solutions

Monitor and evaluate your progress

Remember, Guilt Can Work For You

[Three Strategies for Forgiving Ourselves For What We Have Done To Ourselves](#)

[Define Your Remorse](#)

[Detach From Your Guilt for a Moment](#)

[Reconcile with yourself](#)

[Three Strategies For Forgiving Ourselves For What We Have Done To Others](#)

[Admit to Yourself](#)

[Switch places with the hurt person](#)

[Absolve yourself from the guilt](#)

[Chapter 8: Proven Strategies for Overcoming Feelings of Guilt with Others](#)

[Acknowledge and Apologize](#)

[Make Amends Quickly](#)

[Change Your Behavior](#)

[Accept and Move On](#)

[Overcoming Guilt in the Company of Others](#)

[Three Strategies That Allow Others to Forgive Us for What We Have Done to Ourselves](#)

[Appreciate the complexity of human behavior](#)

[Evoke empathy and compassion](#)

[Express your past trauma](#)

Three Strategies That Allow Others to Forgive Us for What We Have Done to Them

Remind them that human is to err

Express your good intentions went bad

Mention that you didn't know better

Chapter 9: How to Prevent Self-Loathing from Returning

How to Avoid Guilt and Keep It Away

Avoid setting unrealistic standards or expectations

Only make those promises you can keep

Don't entertain self-blame

Stop using guilt as a motivation or punishment tool

Prioritize Tasks

Build a Long-term Battle plan

The Need To Remove Those Things Which Remind You of Guilt

How to Forget Things on Purpose

Dangers of ruminating on bad memories

How to tackle unwanted memories

Know when it's happening

Expose yourself to possible triggers

Set aside some 'me time.'

Practice mindfulness

Try Self-Acceptance

The Need for Mantras to Manage Your Guilt

What do mantras entail?

Mantras for Depression

Mantras for Anxiety

Mantras for Mental Clarity

Soothing Mantras

Chapter 10: People Who Inhibit Your Self-Forgiveness

Example 1

Example 2

The Narcissism Epidemic

Shifting the blame onto you

Ridiculing you

Gaslighting

Deflecting arguments

The People Who Make You Feel Guilty Are Immoral Themselves

It would help if you cut the haters from your life

Haters at Home

Haters at Work

Online Haters

Three Strategies for Dealing With Your Haters

Step 1: Consider The Mindset Behind The Hate

Is it constructive criticism or hate?

It's not personal. Nothing is!

What kind of mental space are you responding from?

You NEVER have to fight for your worth.

Step 2: Check In Emotionally

Step 3: Action Time

Conclusion

(1) Recognition

(2) Responsibility

(3) Expression

(4) Rebirth

Understand your guilt

Move Past Guilt

Introduction

Are you ashamed of doing or saying something you shouldn't have?

Do you think it is your fault when things go wrong, and you cannot seem to forgive yourself no matter how much you try?

Do you want to rise above your past mistakes but cannot seem to let go of the guilt?

If this is you, I'm here to tell you that you don't have to live this way!

This book will help you dig deeper into your thoughts and feelings and see why you can't easily forgive yourself. The strategies in this book will help you discover if an unfortunate event was truly your fault or not and show you how to free yourself from the blame, anger, guilt, and shame you feel right now.

Each of us has said or done some things we are not so proud of or wish would have turned out differently. Maybe you forgot your husband's birthday, failed to pick up your child from school, criticized someone's career path, spoke thoughtlessly, bullied others, used up half the rent to buy new clothes, had an affair, and the list goes on.

Feeling bad knowing what we've done is wrong is something we all do. The problem is losing ourselves in those bad feelings or wallowing in guilt. Instead of owning up to what we've done and making things right, we can unconsciously start using self-blame or guilt to punish ourselves for our wrongs and fuel unforgivingness.

But why is unforgivingness so bad? It can negatively impact our thoughts, behaviors, emotions, body, and spirit. The unbearable pain from the scars of betrayal, fear, rejection, and insecurity causes bitterness, resentment, and even revenge if not addressed.

Unforgivingness fuels overthinking which then infiltrates our rational minds. We can start pondering every question asked or decision made in life and consider them all a mistake or even deliberate. As we continue digging up, analyzing, and mentally replaying every negative experience, we refresh the pain we felt. Consequently, we do not let time heal wounds but instead worsen and afflict more emotional pain on ourselves.

Unforgivingness can compare to a massive load on your shoulders—the longer you carry it, the heavier it becomes.

Your pain becomes more harrowing when you start worrying over what you could have done differently to prevent it or thinking that you had other options but chose the wrong one.

In short, nurturing unforgivingness is toxic and can affect many aspects of your life, including work performance, school, marriage, and relationships. The guilt can make you seem withdrawn, less open, and more critical than you usually are. Everybody around you—your children, spouse, parents, friends, even your dog—can suffer with you.

Furthermore, numerous studies have suggested that people who have difficulty forgiving are more likely to suffer from high blood pressure, heart attacks, malignant tumors, depression, sleep deprivation, mental health problems, anxiety, and other illnesses. And, if you continue watering the negativity, your brain can start producing chemicals that can destroy your vital body organs. So, in hindsight, unforgivingness can ruin your life.

Therefore, prioritizing forgiveness, especially for self, is paramount to healing and restoration. On the other hand, trying to forget and go on with life as if nothing is wrong with your behavior shows denial. To alleviate these effects of unforgivingness, you need the restorative power of self-forgiveness.

But what does self-forgiveness entail?

Forgiving yourself implies admitting that you have deliberately or accidentally hurt others or yourself, apologizing, and being ready to forge ahead. It means you intentionally choose to continue with life despite the offense, free from the disgrace, anger, and other accompanying emotions. Therefore, forgiving yourself doesn't show weakness or that you condone your negative behaviors or want to get off the hook for whatever you said or did. Instead, self-forgiveness calls for introspection, understanding, compassion, and empathy for self and others.

Self-forgiveness also compels you to explore hidden perceptions, patterns, trauma, and reactions that could thwart your efforts to absolve guilt. As you explore the situation with an open mind, you can see the pain you caused and even feel obliged to look for ways to heal it. In return, whenever you let yourself or others down, you will choose to understand and offer yourself some kindness instead of criticizing yourself.

As you start practicing self-forgiveness, remember that;

Self-forgiveness is a process

Self-forgiveness is not a one-time event but a process that unfolds over time through self-reflection and emotional work. By engaging in self-forgiveness, you seek to attain a balance between accepting responsibility and maintaining a good self-image. Once you achieve this balance, you will be able to forgive yourself.

As will be illustrated in this book, genuine self-forgiveness has three fundamental aspects;

Expressing unpleasant feelings directed toward yourself

When you do something harmful, inappropriate, or against your principles, you may experience painful, negative emotions such as shame, remorse, resentment, or wrath. You may also form wrong attitudes such as, "It's all my fault," or "I'm a horrible person."

Remorse may be beneficial since it motivates us to make apologies. Self-forgiveness doesn't quite mean that we skip the stage of feeling awful; instead, we process these emotions of self-resentment and then let them go once they've served their function.

Developing good feelings directed toward yourself

Self-forgiveness cultivates emotions and thoughts toward oneself in the form of self-compassion, love, and kindness, in addition to placing our destructive emotions behind us. We may recognize our shared humanity and realize that we are all flawed and make errors by practicing self-compassion

Accepting responsibility

Recognizing the "wrongness" of your conduct is required for true self-forgiveness. It is "pseudo-self-forgiveness" if your only goal is to absolve yourself of negative feelings and make you happy. You should consider the happiness of the person you hurt, not just yours.

Pay attention to how the person you hurt feels, apologize and recommit to your principles. I believe that doing so will make it less likely for you to repeat the mistake.

There are also four steps you should follow to reach genuine self-forgiveness;

The 4 Rs Of Self-Forgiveness

Essentially, forgiving yourself has four sequential steps or actions as follows;

Responsibility

To take responsibility, you need to face the situation, agree it was wrong, and be accountable for the hurtful things you are responsible for to lessen the negative emotions. You stop excusing, justifying, or downplaying your actions and recognize the part you played.

Remorse

Accepting responsibility may arouse unpleasant feelings like guilt, blame, or shame. Such feelings can drive behavior change besides serving as a warning. So, don't worry; feeling that way is normal and healthy.

Restoration

Another important self-forgiveness milestone is seeking restoration. You somehow try to patch up things. Forgiving yourself becomes sustainable when you know you deserve it. In the same way, you cannot forgive others until they somehow compensate for doing you wrong.

To resolve the problem, start by apologizing to those you hurt. It might seem like apologies only benefit the offended, but you also gain something too —at least you will never wonder if you did your best.

Renewal

Make a comeback free from emotional burdens. Stop the self-hatred and revamp your motivation and self-confidence, ready to face whatever problem life throws at you.

I could just tell you to embrace self-forgiveness now, but it is not as easy as you think.

Why Is It Hard To Forgive Yourself?

First, some of us struggle with self-forgiveness because we refuse to approve of it and prefer to suffer endlessly in guilt to punish ourselves for transgressions. We perhaps view self-forgiveness as giving ourselves a pass to continue our destructive behavior. Perfectionists and narcissists are incapable of forgiving themselves because they firmly refuse to recognize and accept that they make mistakes.

Second, escaping the negative cycle of emotions isn't a walk in the park—because of the underlying negative thoughts. Negative thinking may rapidly become ingrained. The more we think negatively, the better we grow at it. Paying attention to our negative thoughts is easy because we cannot escape them. If I repeatedly tell you not to think about something, all you will think about is that thing!

Even when you know something is not great for you, it's tough to quit thinking about it. Considering how easy it becomes a habit, you may enter a never-ending negative thought cycle. Furthermore, mental illnesses like depression may cause negative thinking, increasing the condition's intensity. Hence, the never-ending spiral of negativity.

Lastly, the pressure, inside and outside, could be a stumbling block. As we will learn later, the people in our life can keep us stuck in the self-blame cycle by constantly finding ways to make us feel guilty.

Self-forgiveness somehow forces you to zoom in on how you deal with yourself when wrong.

Are you often critical, harsh, or unforgiving, or do you pardon yourself?

Do you let your inner critic get the best of you? Perhaps even telling yourself you don't deserve forgiveness for anything, or often give others more leeway for lousy behavior but hold yourself to an unbelievably high standard (where you must be perfect). As a Psychology Today article suggests, our anxiety can be rooted in fear of making mistakes and seeming imperfect. This fear forces us to want to appear immaculate with no dirt or baggage in front of others. And, as we try to portray our best to others, we live by their expectations, not ours.

Why Should We Embrace Self-Forgiveness?

Self-forgiveness allows you to stay accountable without victimizing yourself. It also promotes extra self-acceptance and compassion that enables you to carefully observe your emotions and thoughts with a non-judgmental attitude, accept them, and finally let go of them, replacing them with trust and self-love. Once you stop seeing yourself as a bad person, you regain confidence and self-belief.

Some other benefits include the following;

- Improved mental health
- Less anxiety, hostility, and stress
- Improved heart health
- Lessened depression symptoms
- Decrease blood pressure
- A stronger immune system
- Healthier relationships

As demonstrated, you stand to gain a lot from forgiving yourself. And although it could be an uncomfortable, painful process, forgiving yourself is worth it.

So, if you are tired of living with unnecessary self-sabotaging beliefs and self-criticism and seeking a road to more understanding, healing, and inner peace, you have picked the right book.

In this book, you will discover;

- The root causes of guilt and self-blame – some will shock you

- What you will gain once you eventually forgive yourself, along with the risks of not doing so

- Why it may not be entirely your fault, and exactly how to stop thinking so

- Simple, helpful self-forgiveness practices you can start implementing right away to feel less stressed and uneasy

- How to swiftly forgive yourself even for the seemingly unforgivable acts

- Why don't have to forget to heal from an offense completely

- How to remain empathetic and apologize to those you hurt after forgiving yourself

- Why proper timing is critical to self-forgiveness

Plus, much more!

You don't have to wallow in unforgivingness and a miserable life of self-blame and shame. Jump on to the next chapter and discover how to break this debilitating cycle.

Chapter 1: It's Not Your Fault. Stop Dealing With It.

Like most people, you may blame yourself for things you did not do or are not your fault. When things go wrong, do you often say, 'it's all my fault," "I should have, would have, and could have done this or that," or suffer an endless sense of shame or guilt?

Of course, taking responsibility for something that has let others down shows maturity. And, it is okay to feel bad when we fail ourselves and others in ordinary things like a failed project or a missed deadline. But it is unrealistic to blame it all on you or stay fixated on the wrong.

Although self-blame and guilt are intrinsic, they are attitudes we pick from everyday experiences. So, thinking it is all your fault is not an inborn trait but something we acquire from our surroundings, especially when we are children.

Both are negative self-conscious emotions triggered by wrongdoing or shortcomings. If left unresolved, the worthlessness stirred by shame or guilt can trigger addiction, aggression, depression, and other destructive reactions.

Before we move to why you feel that way, let's first explore the following;

Telltale Signs of Self-Blame

Toxic self-criticism

One of the signs of self-blame is that you suffer toxic self-criticism.

Suppose some people in your life openly criticized, blamed you unjustly, or gave you unrealistic standards. In that case, you may internalize their judgments or expectations which affect how you view the world and yourself.

You may often think:

- I'm worthless.

- I'm always wrong,
- I'm not good enough.
- I did something to set it off.
- I still feel like I've failed, even if I don't know why.
- I made things worse by not noticing it earlier.

Such false beliefs can be draining and indicate you have low twisted self-esteem. They can arise from perfectionism issues, like having impossible, unachievable standards.

Some people are highly self-critical.

When faced with relationship difficulties, some people blame themselves and say awful things to themselves. For example, I have encountered people whose divorces happened long ago. However, they still blame themselves for certain things that ended their union and struggle with marriage loss years later.

At times, they blame their failure to notice some of their ex-partner's problems that could have been present way back when they were dating. They end up convincing themselves that they initially saw signals of marriage failure but ignored them. So they are somehow to blame for the shame caused by that unforgivable initial error.

Others blamed themselves without recognizing their partner's role in how things turned out. They completely trust the accusations poured at them, although one or both of them played a part in the failure of their marriage, and it could have been solely the ex's fault.

Some go to the extent of defending domestic violence with statements like;

"One day, my ex-husband came home drunk and beat me up, which was unusual. I may have provoked him somehow with my loud mouth when I reflect on that day."

In short, self-criticism is partly owed to our unrealistic belief that we must be perfect. Any signs of imperfection initiate self-criticism and blame for actual or apparent failure—low self-worth, incompetence, insecurity, trail such thinking. Therefore, we should embrace self-compassion and forgiveness instead.

Black-and-white thinking

This kind of thinking makes you think in extremes. There is no middle ground. There is no other way. You may feel that you always fail or never do anything well and regularly do wrong. Others are better than you, and everything about you is inaccurate.

Such an attitude can paralyze you and get you stuck in life. It can result in projecting all your good qualities onto others—considering them flawless and you as the monster.

Chronic self-doubt

You could have many doubts and negative thoughts, such as,

Am I doing things right?

Is it enough?

Can I make it? I always seem to fail.

Could I be right?

I know I tend to think terribly and overreact sometimes, but could it be true this time?

Unfulfilling relationships

When self-blame or guilt manifests in your relationships, you may seem to assume a lot of responsibilities and even get exploited. In interpersonal or romantic relationships, you may tolerate abuse and consider it as usual. You could be incapable of constructively resolving conflicts or have a weird perspective of how healthy relationships look.

Interpersonal problems such as people-pleasing, codependency, Stockholm syndrome, learned helplessness, poor boundaries, inability to decline any offer, and self-destruction could also arise.

Self-harm and poor self-care

When overly self-critical, we can automatically blame ourselves for getting hurt and be susceptible to poor self-care or self-harm.

Growing up, you may have lacked love, care, and protection and found it challenging to care for yourself. Therefore, you may often feel unworthy of having your needs met. You can end up blaming or harming yourself unconsciously as a punishment for wrongdoing, as you learned as a child. Caring for others' needs could even seem nobler.

The Causes of Self-Blame

There are many underlying reasons you may engage in self-blame or guilt when bad things happen.

Below are some of these reasons:

Unresolved Trauma

Bullying, disasters, early childhood problems, violence, physical abuse, etc., are all traumas. Therapists suggest that trauma victims mostly blame themselves as a defense mechanism against feeling powerless over their traumatic experiences.

They also propose that many of us usually suffer mild or complex symptoms of unresolved trauma like self-blame, unreasonable anger, recurring flashbacks, bad memories, and sleeplessness. Out of all these symptoms, self-blame is one of the most toxic. This self-blame hinders the possibility of healing and recovering from trauma.

I'd primarily cite conscious or unconscious developmental conditioning as the underlying issue behind trauma-related guilt.

So, I will discuss two broad causes of traumas that cause guilt;

- *Past Conditioning*

Our nervous system is like our internal alarm. Unaware, it constantly looks out for any danger around us. When it is triggered, it goes off, and we then quickly assess the situation and decide whether to escape, fight, run or hide.

Therefore, when we encounter a traumatic event, we are programmed to respond in specific ways unconsciously. Unfortunately, we are mostly unaware of these near-instant scans and automated responses.

This obliviousness can make us assume that there is something more we could have done to prevent the bad stuff from happening, consequently feeling guilty and blaming ourselves. The truth is that we do everything to safeguard ourselves, even when things go wrong.

You may be conditioned from childhood to own up for things that are not your responsibility. Some of us come from dysfunctional families and bring that dysfunction to our adult lives. The trauma could have been so profound that you made it your own.

You could have experienced emotional, mental, or physical abuse you took as your fault to demonstrate the shame or worthlessness you felt. You may have been treated that way (scapegoated or guilted) by a significant person in your formative years, which became your automatic response. Or, maybe you had a romantic relationship with people who deflect blame on you and were unaccountable for their hurtful behavior—look within to identify the wiring of your neurons.

- *Physical, Emotional, Or Sexual Abuse*

According to psychologists, sexually/physically abused people can assume responsibility for whatever happened and blame themselves for their offender's behavior or character (e.g., "I was weak." "I drank a little too much." "I deserved punishment." "I should have strongly fought back."

If, for instance, you suffered sexual abuse as a child or young adult, you might grow to believe that you were responsible for the perpetrator's wrong behavior and cannot recognize that you were simply the victim of their manipulation.

Furthermore, suppose, as a child, you were mistreated, abandoned, or lost a sole breadwinner or loved one. Your naive brain may think it is because of something you somehow did; it's your entire fault. Your brain can take this assumption as accurate (what psychologists call a 'core belief'). It will then apply to any other complex thing you face in life.

Additionally, parenting that prevents us from being ourselves could trigger self-blame. If, for example, your parents showed you love only when you were 'quiet' or 'good' but criticized, ignored, or punished you when you had a different opinion, were sad or angry, then you would believe you have this 'bad side.' If you let that side out, whatever goes wrong is 'entirely your fault.'

Moreover, if your parents or relatives blamed you as a child for feeling hurt and told you things like,

- ☐ *That shouldn't make you mad.*
- ☐ *You are lying.*
- ☐ *Look at what you made me do.*
- ☐ *It does not hurt.*
- ☐ *Stop making things up.*
- ☐ *If you don't behave nicely, I'll go and leave you here alone.*
- ☐ *I will give you something real to cry about.*

That is the opposite of what a sad child (or anyone else) needs. It makes us unfairly blame ourselves for whatever happened and suppress our real feelings because;

We cannot see our caregivers' flaws and wounds when we are young. At that age, we cannot step outside what's happening and see that although they love us, our caregivers cannot meet our every need. We can't see past ourselves, so it is impossible to blame someone else since we cannot assign blame that pain must go somewhere, often inward.

Self-blame is a survival tool. Assigning blame to your guardian can make you see that they may be imperfect and incapable of looking after you entirely. Doing so can imply we are all alone in a world where nobody can care for us. Blaming ourselves helps us feel in control and safe -even if we're not.

Away from trauma, let us explore some other causes of 'it is my fault syndrome'.

Depression

When depressed, you may feel inadequate and blame yourself for your failures resulting in feelings of hopelessness and helplessness. Depression can ultimately erode our confidence, intensify feelings of shame and relentless self-blame, and feed the self-blame cycle.

Albeit depression is an illness, we may find ourselves caught up in the process of self-beating and self-blaming for our condition. We can start blaming ourselves for getting depression.

Thoughts like "I am depressed about losing my job, and it was all my fault," or 'If I weren't lazy, I would have been cured of depression by now."

If you mull over this for a long time, you can start coming up with so many reasons why being depressed is your fault.

You should first of all realize that depression is not your fault. It's a mental health condition with various causes, some biological, others environmental, and can trigger a negative spiral of complicated thoughts. That could be why you appear anti-social or behave in a manner you wouldn't want when well— perhaps being more irritable, snapping at others for no reason, and beating yourself up for doing so.

Please don't assume that any depression symptom is your fault. Because you are essentially out of character, you could behave out of character. Although depression should not be an excuse – and apologies are noble when we hurt others— it could overwhelm situations and intimidate you more if you are a victim. You may find socializing too much to handle, sleeping more than others, and persistently angry. Try to give yourself some kindness.

Instead of self-blame or guilt, there are healthier ways to cope with your heightened emotional state, such as attending therapy, consulting a doctor, taking prescribed medication, improving your self-care, etc. But now, you need to accept that you can't simply snap your fingers and instantly become depression-free.

Anxiety

Anxiety and guilt are co-dependent— they form a vicious cycle: Anxiety triggers guilt, which sequentially creates more stress. For instance, you can fear being scrutinized by others if you have a social anxiety disorder (SAD). It can make you worry that you could have said the wrong stuff, spoken unkindly, or yelled, so it is your fault someone is hurt, your work is of poor quality, and so on.

Being overly self-critical and judgmental, you suffer guilt or shame even for mistakes that are not your fault. You overthink various things and frantically examine others' expressions, gestures, tones, and words, which is exhausting. It can make you feel on edge, irritable, defensive, sorrowful, and desperate to say sorry and improve the situation.

Other symptoms include over-apologizing, clinginess, over-compensating for the invented offense, over-pleasing others, and evading judgment. You wrongly assume that you are responsible for making others happy and are at fault for their problems.

Obsessive-Compulsive Disorder(OCD)

Suppose you suffer from obsessive behaviors or thinking. You may be so obsessed with your behavior/thoughts that your fears intensify. In that case, to avoid being blamed, you can carefully tend to engage in some weird behaviors to prevent any future liability.

For instance, say you are late to work and, while driving, you spot a trash bag in the middle of the road. What would you do?

As an ordinary person (without OCD), you may veer off it and continue driving to avoid being late to work. Afterward, you will most likely get busy with your day and completely forget the trash bag.

But if you have OCD, you may initially veer off and continue driving to avoid being late for work. But the trash bag will come to mind during the day again. You may think that if an accident occurs because a driver fails to see the bag in time, it would be entirely your fault. It would not matter to you that many people could have seen and ignored the trash bag too. The whole thing is all your fault.

You can become obsessed with the fear of a looming accident. Ask your coworkers if they saw the trash bag, trying to establish that you are not an awful person for not moving it. Perhaps compulsively pray for forgiveness if religious. You can even go back to the spot to find out if it has caused an accident. You get fixated on fearing that if anybody gets hurt, then you are to blame.

This incessant self-blame can also put people off as you don't allow them to take responsibility for their wrongs and patch them up. Once they withdraw from you, you could feel lonely, terrible, shameful, and more at fault. And the cycle goes on.

To end this cycle, you need to realize that you are not responsible for some things, and some bad things can occur without your interference.

In summary:

Guilt and self-blame are illogical responses that could be deeply rooted in sources that might not be your fault and are hard to elude. You could be responding to a traumatic experience that is not your fault - you didn't ask for it nor want it.

We turn to self-blame or guilt as an alternative to relieve anxiety and other related emotions and feel soothed. It also strengthens our limiting beliefs and unworthiness, somehow endorsing our right to self-hate and self-blame. Self-blame and guilt hinder healing from your past and promote self-destructiveness. We seem subconsciously fixed on continuing to hurt ourselves. Holding onto mistakes long after they happen and everyone else has moved on. To avoid opening up past wounds, you can redirect your energy to accusing, criticizing, and beating yourself up. You can become distracted from the other problems and pains you have.

What factors are at play inside you?

I have only highlighted the major underlying factors of self-blame and guilt. If yours differs from these categories, as our experiences are different and complicated, seek the help of an experienced therapist to explore your narrative and perception.

Generally, guilt is of two kinds: "healthy" and "unhealthy." Knowing the type of guilt you feel helps you handle it appropriately.

Healthy guilt is that nasty feeling that comes after you know you have indeed misbehaved—for instance, after hurting someone or causing an avoidable problem. That guilt tells you to say sorry and be good next time. It can also indicate your great empathy and moral or ethical standards.

However, we sometimes feel irrationally guilty for things that are entirely not our fault. And this is an unhealthy kind of guilt. If you fail to manage it, you go down a negative spiral. The negative thinking resulting from depression, OCD, burnout, etc., causes severe health issues, reinforcing unhealthy guilt.

Moving on:

The Three Strategies for Letting Go of Unhealthy Guilt

We will cover healthy guilt in a later chapter to avoid repetition. To help you with the unhealthy guilt, let's look at the simple strategies you can use:

Be realistic about what is controllable

To begin, think about and list whatever you can control in a situation. Create another list of those things you can't. If you write a longer second list, your guilt is probably baseless and unhelpful. Remember to be only answerable for your behavior, not for others' thoughts or actions.

Ignore the stuff that you can't realistically control. Concentrate on the circumstances you can resolve. Where applicable, plan for the solution.

For instance, millions globally lost their jobs because of COVID-19; some of us felt a little guilty that we survived, and others didn't (aka survivor guilt.)

In this case, accepting you were somehow 'lucky' for surviving and empathizing with those who didn't is okay. However, trying to instantly snap out of it and move on as if it didn't exist is somehow lying to yourself. But it would be best to avoid wallowing in guilt as it would be a needless burden.

In its place, you can gather the emotions behind the guilt and direct them to do something good for the victims. Such a positive response empowers you to take control of the situation rather than feel helpless.

For example, someone could appreciate you more for being there, listening, accepting, and accompanying them throughout their distressing situations. You can make a difference by simply enquiring about what others need.

Once you find purpose as things go wrong, it converts guilt into a sincere appreciation for success. You can then try seizing the day by making the best of your "blessing" – utilize the opportunity rather than wallow in guilt.

Use affirmations

Secondly, you can deal with the constant repetitive unjustified guilty feelings by silencing your negative self-talk and gathering others' opinions to get an unbiased viewpoint. Follow this up with short affirmations confirming what happened isn't your fault.

Once you recognize the parts you could control in the situation, use simple positive statements. For example, *"I was promoted before Erick because of my top-notch skills and experience,"* rather than, *"I got this promotion because I was so pushy and over-ambitious."*

Restate your words and tell yourself a different story.

A helpful affirmation for various situations would be, "I did my best using the knowledge I had at the time." At the end of this chapter, you will find more affirmations you can say out loud or intone after you stumble.

Challenge perfectionism

As discussed, setting unrealistic standards for yourself could arouse a guilty response if they are unmet. You can suffer guilt about not doing it or seeming inadequate, even if you were not responsible for their failure. Just like that, you may overlook anything you have already done well.

Reflect on any perfectionist behaviors and challenge them to keep your standards realistic. After all – being human is to err!

To stop the self-blame caused by perfectionism;

Do your best to avoid being distracted by slight errors or superficial imperfections. Use realistic optimism to change your negative thoughts to cope with challenges. Change "I always blunder!" to "When I make mistakes, I can fix some but can't fix others." "I feel proud of myself."

"I am great at everything I do!" is too general and unrealistic. Try to be specific when affirming yourself.

Be assertive with those who instill guilt for no reason

Someone trying to control you can put unrealistic pressure on you or deliberately arouse guilt in you. Some people may turn things around, putting you at fault for a wrong you did not commit as they deflect the blame or attention away (like narcissists). They try to make you feel guilty about doing what they want.

Consider a supervisor who constantly asks his teammates to work overtime for the team's sake – but on the other hand, he implies that those seeking a work-life balance are "not good team players." His actions can trigger guilt in you for no good reason.

Therefore, assert yourself in such situations and speak your mind confidently if you're not in the wrong.

It would help if you reminded yourself continually that;

You are to do an excellent job in everything you embark on but not to make people happy. We are responsible for our happiness. So you should only own up to actions you are responsible for, not just anything happening in your life.

This way, you take the responsibility you can discharge to your satisfaction without the extra pressure and external threats. You are better off saying 'No' from the onset rather than regretting it later.

While at it, consider using affirmations.

These are essentially self-declarations asserting your abilities. Researchers propose that affirmations stimulate brain changes and activate your brain's reward center. They work partly because our subconscious cannot quickly tell apart real and imagined experiences. You can come up with personalized affirmations, but ensure they are not too long and focus on core values or positive experiences for the best results. Also, " Stay present using " I am." "I have" not "I will" in your statements.

As promised, here are the following;

30 Affirmations to help reduce negativity and to enable you to embrace and love yourself even when you feel unworthy of it;

1. I am compassionate toward others and myself.
2. I let go of whatever does not serve me.
3. I'm improving all the time.
4. I release negative emotions and thoughts. They have entirely gone!
5. I am courageous, and I stand up for myself.
6. I am no longer wounded. Now I am healed.
7. I choose to live in a way that brings peace, happiness, and joy to myself and others.
8. Today is the start of whatever I want.
9. I love to smile; it is my gift to the world.
10. I choose to enjoy this day.
11. I release old feelings quickly, letting them pass all out.
12. I am doing my best every day.
13. I have unconditional love for myself and the world.
14. I quickly release feelings of shame or guilt.
15. I'm moving on, so goodbye, past nonsense!

16. I see the good in myself and others.
17. I feel grateful and uplifted.
18. I accept 100% responsibility for my own life.
19. Mistakes are teachers. I take the lessons they offer.
20. I am full of grace.
21. I choose to be positive.
22. I am in charge of my happiness.
23. Every day, in every way, I slide into that better version of myself.
24. I Inhale confidence and exhale doubt.
25. I love myself for who I am.
26. My actions complement my intentions every day.
27. Today is a new day, and I start it with gratitude.
28. Radiant energy vibrates through my whole body.
29. If I feel guilty, it's probably just gaslighting.
30. The people who blame most are themselves to blame.

There you go with enough affirmations to get you started. Meanwhile, keep reading because we'll explore more safe ways to heal ourselves from such negativity later. So, hold onto your hope. Help is on the way.

But first, even after realizing that your past experiences, earlier brainwashing, or underlying mental disorder could trigger your behavior and make you prone to making mistakes, you could still hold that everything is your fault. Let's explain why it may be so in the next chapter.

Chapter 2: Maybe It Was Your Fault. That's okay.

Self-blame is often not about accepting responsibility. Instead, it is an unconscious attempt to avoid facing the truth of the situations we find ourselves in. By taking responsibility, you effortlessly bypass any further discussion or examination of what occurred.

Furthermore, always assuming that everything is your fault is also a form of self-abuse. You subject yourself to so much guilt and shame that it paralyzes you, preventing you from growing and changing.

You may wonder if it is so bad, then;

Why can't you stop thinking, 'It's All My Fault?

Maybe the reason self-blame is hard to stop is that it can be pretty addictive. Addictions flourish when used as a way to cope with emotional pain. Plus, there are some hidden ways you could benefit through self-blame.

As many life coaches suggest, we must first accept its benefits to stop any habit. If all self-blame does is make us feel stuck and lonely, why would we possibly continue to use it? Are there benefits to taking the blame?

You get to feel sorry for yourself

When you blame yourself, you victimize yourself. It's a backward way to go into 'poor me' mode.

You gain attention

And when we feel sorry for ourselves, it forces others to feel sorry for us, too. It might not be the best way to get attention, but it does the trick.

You maintain control

It could be hard to accept, but striving always to claim responsibility is borderline manipulative. You constantly block the other person from deciding how things will go and use sympathy to ensure they don't pull away and leave you.

It gives you power

It could be hard to believe when you have such low self-esteem that you'd want power over another. But low self-esteem can mean we want the ability to stop others from hurting or abandoning us. This means always claiming it's all my fault ends up as a way to have control over others.

You can avoid changing

If we always take the blame, we don't have to experience new emotions or conversations.

You don't have to be vulnerable

As for an abused person, accepting someone else has perhaps wronged you (even if they did not mean to) can force you to put yourself in a place where you feel vulnerable and hurt. Using self-blame means you resort to shame as opposed to showing vulnerability.

The price of always taking the blame

Constant self-blame is a reverse psychological projection. Usually, through self-projection, we bestow the qualities we don't like onto another person to avoid seeing them in ourselves. You also project your good and bad traits. Suddenly they are the dishonest ones, the rude ones, etc.

However, claiming exclusive responsibility prevents the other person from providing their perspective on the incident. They cannot accept responsibility and evolve due to what has occurred.

So the other person frequently becomes agitated, feels imprisoned, and withdraws. Your relationships are locked in an often dramatic routine of blaming one other and pleading for forgiveness rather than working through issues together and forging genuine connections.

The result? You feel lonely, unwanted, and even more like a dreadful, awful person who is constantly to blame. So, the cycle goes on.

So, yes, you think it's your fault, but have you considered it may not entirely be so and that you may not be solely responsible for your mistakes?

Even Things That Seem Like Your Fault Probably Aren't

It would help if you considered other correlated circumstances, events, or factors you cannot control that can come into play instead of criticizing yourself when bad things happen.

To get what this means, look at the following examples;

Example 1: If sales are down in your business or if it's headed for closure, you may feel exclusively at fault as the manager or owner, but you are not. Other factors beyond your control could trigger low sales.

Maybe it's the bad weather, the construction nearby, the presence of new competitors, or unfavorable business climate like raised taxes, Covid restrictions, suppliers' increased prices, leading to increased product prices which are less competitive, etc.

Although you should be true to yourself and not mindlessly blame the competition, employees, or any other changing variables, identifying and acknowledging that many other factors could come into play and lead to a problem is essential.

If, as a good entrepreneur, you have tried to adjust and rise above the issues affecting your business and sales don't seem to improve, it would be unfair to feel guilty for closing it down or blame it solely on your inefficient management ability.

Example 2: Say you are experiencing problems in your relationships and cannot work things out. Try to identify external circumstances, influences, or stuff you may be dealing with to understand why everything seems to head south.

Avoid feeling guilty or blaming yourself, thinking it is entirely your fault. Plus, don't be afraid to call out your partner or any person for whatever they do wrong that negatively affects your relationship. With that said, let us examine some situations that could provoke problems — that have nothing to do with you.

Sometimes, after an argument, you can do everything possible to work things out, including apologizing—much honor to you for holding up your end. But the other party should also join in. It is not your fault if they are hurt but unwilling to admit the part they played and adjust their behavior.

So it may not be your fault that someone;

- Doesn't want to listen.

- Is not apologizing; you are the only one doing it.

- Remains moody constantly, gets bad-tempered when you talk, or regularly shuts you up.

- Is experiencing a different stage in life with other priorities; you don't match up.

- Is not open to criticism, unlike you, who is making progress.

- Is quick to point fingers at you for everything going wrong.

- Has money problems.

- Is jealous for no reason.

- Or has unrealistic expectations.

Note: *These issues can manifest in relationships with colleagues, family members, and friends, making us feel at fault for hurting them when we shouldn't.*

Even so,

Some sources are more likely to be the cause than others.

Some issues in life can make you unnecessarily feel at fault if you are not careful. Here is a non-comprehensive list of familiar everyday problems that can make us feel inadequate, and we end up blaming ourselves unfairly when they happen:

Financial crisis

We live in a world full of uncertainty, mainly regarding financial matters. We are bound to experience financial crises at one point or the other. While it is good to anticipate a financial crisis and stay prepared, it could come unexpectedly or hit stronger than you expected.

For instance, unemployment, a common societal problem that could happen unexpectedly, can make you feel guilty for not doing anything all day. One day, my neighbor shared that he had been unemployed and never told anybody. He said that the worst time was when he woke up in the morning; he was too ashamed to leave his apartment and felt imprisoned until five in the afternoon, when he would typically leave work. He didn't want anyone to know he was unemployed.

Actually, in Tokyo, some people dress in suits early in the morning, leave their houses, take a train to a different part of the city, sit all day in a park and return home in the evening. For many, unemployment brings a feeling of shame, failure, and guilt. It is sad—but human.

As illustrated, you may lose your job due to a financial crisis or lose your investment or savings in a significant lawsuit, or lose your livelihood in a major disaster, which is not your fault.

Health crisis

Another life-changing problem is a health crisis. Sometimes we get sick. Sometimes it is because of something we can control, like poor lifestyle choices, but sometimes, we have no control over our body malfunctions. Some illnesses or infections can occur naturally, like inherited ones, airborne and mental diseases, etc., and cause us to feel bad.

Boredom and emptiness

Another significant impact in your life is when you are in a rut. As you feel empty and bored, you become unexcited about everything. It can make you unproductive, dull, and problematic; you can snap in anger and hurt others.

Confusion

Mental changes can confuse and make you unable to think with your usual clarity. You become more forgetful and may not fully concentrate on tasks, therefore prone to error and hurting yourself and others. Today, confusion is a pressing issue that affects millions. Environmental and medical factors can cause it or an occurrence of heartbreak, loss, or abuse.

Friendship problems

It's good to have friends to hang out with, get our minds off things, and bail us out of trouble. However, many of us have been in big problems due to our friends, e.g., friends who have lied about us, backstabbed us, betrayed our trust, or became jealous of us and told our secrets to everyone.

Such bad experiences can create trust issues that haunt future friendships and cause us to hurt our friends while trying to protect ourselves.

Haunting past

We all have a past we are not so proud of. But sometimes, our past haunts us big time. Worse, your past mistakes may haunt you forever and give you no peace.

Safety and security

Suppose you live in an environment where you experience life-threatening incidents daily, like murder, police brutality, gun violence, and insurgencies. In that case, you may feel anxious and afraid of being the next victim and behave and reason strangely.

Failure

Nobody is immune to experiencing failure. However, failure can cause great disappointments and slow your progress. But remember that failure is inevitable, and you only need to know how to cope (as shown later) to avoid hurting yourself further.

Grief

Nobody desires to grieve, but we cannot protect ourselves from it. Losing a loved one is very painful. If not well handled, it can make us break down emotionally and hurt ourselves and others.

The Bottom Line

Numerous other things can cause problems without your interference. Circumstances like losing jobs, divorce, sick relatives, fatal accidents involving a loved one, illnesses, earthquakes, avalanches, global warming, wars, etc., are all part of life and may have nothing to do with you.

If your boss fires you and renders you unemployed, remember that many factors can cause unemployment, like government policies, global pandemics, expired contracts, etc. Still, losing your job and being unemployed is not entirely your fault. Also, as a boss, firing someone and rendering them jobless is not your fault; the worker may be inefficient, and the economy may be harsh for business.

So your control over situations that produce bad outcomes is too tiny to affect them. Quit blaming yourself or feeling guilty when there is nothing you could have done to stop the disaster from happening and hurting others.

And if somebody feels terrible for no reason, you are not involved. That's not your fault. You can't control how they think or feel. But remember to remain compassionate and empathetic and let go of the unnecessary burden of guilt and shame.

That said, there are things you should NEVER EVER apologize for, and it would be completely ridiculous to do.

Twelve Things You Must Stop Blaming Yourself For

In the past, I often blamed myself for situations or events over which I had no control. Why? Because I believed I must be at fault for something going wrong because I am technically in charge of my own life. However, as I've progressed through the stages of becoming a "full adult," I've realized that the idea that I'm responsible for everything that happens in my life is false. So now I'm here to tell you unequivocally that there are some things in life that neither you nor I can control, and it's perfectly okay to admit that.

So here are 12 things you shouldn't fault yourself or apologize for because the sooner you do so, the happier you'll be.

Your emotions

So what if you cry a lot, are too concerned, or get too passionate about something that matters to you? There's no such thing as "too much" regarding feelings. The sooner you learn that, the more emotionally healthy you'll be.

The way you handle those emotions

Every one of us handles challenges differently. Do this, write out everything you're thinking in a letter, slam shut that door, and don't feel guilty about it. Go for a run and shut off your phone. Do whatever you need to process what you're going through – and do it unapologetically.

Another person's rejection

It's not your fault that someone doesn't like your hair, your stance on politics, or the way you carry yourself. That's their problem. If you're behaving most authentically, that's all you can do. The right people- those who belong in your life- will accept every part of you.

Little failures and significant failures

We're all human, and it is our nature to make mistakes. It doesn't stop there; it is in our hearts to forgive others for their indiscretions. So if we apply the same logic we extend to other people, it is time we also start developing the same courtesy to ourselves.

Someone else's circumstances

In the well-known romantic comedy, *When Harry Met Sally*, a patron who listened to Meg Ryan order a satisfying lunch famously said, "I'll have what she's having." That, as lovely as it is, is not always possible. Don't compare your story to the story of another person. The personal shame of wishing for what another person has can be too much for a single soul to bear.

Your needs

Because we humans are extraordinarily complex, our requirements will differ vastly. Don't ever be ashamed about your knowledge of what it takes for you to feel fulfilled or blame yourself for requiring certain aspects in a career or relationship that others may not consider necessary.

Your guilty pleasures

There's no shame in binge-watching the Bachelorette while eating a massive bowl of Pad Thai. Enjoying dating, happy hour, or meditating every night is also okay. You like what you like; don't try to hide it.

Being terrible at something

Life is full of trial and error. Some of us were born with the ability to turn an antique coffee table into a work of art, while others can burn themselves with a hot glue gun. You have unique gifts to offer the world different from someone else's.

Putting yourself first before everyone and everything else

You can have the most important relationship with your heart, mind, and soul. There's nothing wrong with being a little selfish when the situation calls for it.

Trusting somebody, you shouldn't have

Feeling damaged or betrayed by someone can consume you, but their actions are entirely their own and have no connection to you.

People have flaws. Sometimes certain flaws are noticeable right away, but sometimes they don't become apparent until years later. If we kept our walls up each time we met someone to avoid getting hurt, we'd live a life of loneliness – and there's nothing worse.

A terminated relationship

Some people were not to remain in our lives forever after they had taught us particular lessons. That's all there is to it.

Whatever happened in the past

Any event, positive or negative, belongs to the period during which it occurred. Ruminating on the past is akin to consciously putting on a puka-shell necklace or any other hideous fashion trend from the previous few years every morning. You can make a conscious decision to live in the present moment. The only direction you can go is forward, which is terrific.

With that out of the way,

Forgiving yourself becomes difficult if you always blame yourself, even when you are not responsible, without considering other factors. When you encounter troubles in life, it is best to try and look for their root cause rather than blaming yourself. Ask yourself; What exactly is the cause of the issues you feel are your fault but are not?

If you still need help finding the root causes of your problems, use the strategies below:

Three Strategies For Finding The Real Causes Of Problems That Seem To Come From You

To stop blaming yourself when the problem is beyond you, use the following strategies to identify the actual cause of your issues;

Analyze your problem

Sometimes we blame ourselves, but we cannot explain why. It would help if you went beyond the story you have told yourself and analyzed your problem in-depth. Reflect on the entire situation to examine what happened. State your issue as is—don't sugarcoat it.

Start by writing down everything that happened and note what you blame yourself for in those problems. Then write down why you blame yourself and give all the details. And as you go further, note down the essential issues —the circumstances related to the event. Add meat to the story.

Why do you blame yourself for that?

You can do this in four columns. You can write the problem in the first column, say business failure. In the second one, write what you blame yourself for, maybe for closing your business down, and in the third column, write why you blame yourself, perhaps because you blame your poor management skills. In the fourth column, write other things that were happening at the time; maybe there was a world economic crisis or global pandemic.

As you write, you may start seeing things differently, realize your issues are far more complicated than you thought, and notice that you had a minor issue that was part of a wide range of related problems.

Eliminate facts from fiction

You may have continually told yourself a story that may not be entirely true, so it is time you re-evaluate your level to separate the lies from the truth. Since our personal stories are usually grounded in hypotheticals, what-if scenarios, and future possibilities, review your account and stick to the facts. When you find yourself stuck in your analysis of the internal stories, unable to take action, try to reason devoid of your emotions and beliefs.

Go over your narrative, trying to see what makes sense—poke holes in the whole report and sieve out the facts of the matter.

Look at your story from an observer's perspective without vested interest or expectations. Ask yourself questions like;

☐ What's factual about this narrative?
☐ What parts of my story are assumptions or hypotheticals?
☐ What parts are entirely untrue?
☐ How much weight are you giving to assumptions?
☐ Are you spending too much time on the theoretical?
☐ What could you have done that could have changed the outcome?

It is time to wake up from the unconscious fantasy you could be making up whenever you face challenges, conflict, and critical issues. Run your findings through a filter of emotions, feelings, thoughts, knowledge, and experiences. Make your observations (what you can perceive using your five senses) in their most authentic sense. Ensure your observations are provable facts and are free of personal bias, judgments, beliefs, or attachments.

Write everything down and go through your new narrative. It could help you see whether you are at fault or not or who or what is truly at fault.

Ask for others' input.

It is easy to get stressed trying to solve problems on our own. Sometimes we can be so caught up in our world that our analysis becomes clouded. You can invite someone you trust or an eyewitness to help you re-examine the situation and give you a different perspective.

You can share your story with that person and express your findings about the situation, or share the story and then listen to their ideas about it. They can give advice that could help you understand that you were not really to blame and that they have observed other things that could have caused the problem. You can use such ideas to help you resolve your issue.

Note: If you can't shake the feeling that everything was your fault, it's time to get help. Trained psychotherapists and counselors could assist you in determining the source of your guilt and self-blame as they provide a secure environment to explore past experiences and repressed emotions. They also help you learn and practice communicating in ways that do not include the default setting of determining everything is your fault.

If indeed, with the help of others, you establish that you certainly played a role in the whole mess, you need to take responsibility, so let's move on to our next point;

Chapter 3: So It Was Your Fault? You're Still a Good Person

At this point, you know that you were responsible for what happened, all other things held constant, and you probably feel like you are the worst person to walk on planet earth. You may be feeling so bad that you even question your morality.

Our past conditioning or flawed perspective about reality may make us think we are evil when we make mistakes. Whatever the case, you must evaluate your thinking and emotions and ground yourself in the truth of the matter that making mistakes doesn't mean you are a terrible person.

After all, since your wrong behavior still bothers you years later, you are a trustworthy person who found yourself in a terrible situation that maybe you haven't forgiven yourself or asked those you hurt for forgiveness.

Some questions you may ask yourself once you know you have erred big time include;

Does feeling guilty for causing a problem prove that you are good?

I would say yes and no in this case.

The fact that you are feeling guilty for doing wrong can mean that you are a good person who went against your conscience. However, feeling guilty doesn't always symbolize or create goodness in you. Many people hurt others and feel bad but continue to do it. *Does that make them good people?*

No, it only means they are ordinary people with guilt instincts. So, the bad feeling you may initially experience when you realize you have probably hurt someone is an ethically neutral signal. It functions as a warning, like pain, to warn you to stop the harm you are inflicting. Once you feel punished enough, you may continue with the same behavior; therefore, you are no better than somebody who ignores the warning sign until it disappears.

In short, guilty feelings may not necessarily have any moral value; they may only serve as signals of bad behavior. Your actions define your morality!

Given that many of us mistake guilt for empathy, let us explore the difference;

Guilt Vs. Empathy

As mentioned earlier, guilt can come from the need for self-atonement from error. We mostly don't look at things from others' perspectives intensely and sensibly enough to trigger empathy, even with strangers. However, empathy entails putting yourself in others' shoes and feeling their pain like it is your own.

So, the intense guilty feeling you feel each time you hurt somebody doesn't symbolize that you are decent or compassionate. Some guilty people can make terrible mistakes to feel rebuked or justified or escape punishment. When you are empathetic, you choose to behave in a way that prevents you from committing a similar offense to others and not for your sake but their sake. Therefore, being punished, forgiven, justified, or atoned is NOT your only goal as an empathetic person.

Feeling guilty is unnecessary as soon as you understand your mistake. Once you realize you were cruel, avoid replaying the scene in your mind or condemning yourself and seek a resolution instead. You need to figure out how not to repeat the mistake in the future (as covered later).

If you hurt someone, focus on working on changing your thoughts or actions to avoid harming others, a.s.a.p. If you offend someone intimate (a lover or friend), apologize and ask them how you can contribute to their healing if possible (if they want nothing to do with you, accept and move on).

Don't try to avoid the person you hurt unless they categorically ask you to leave them alone. Dodging the victim of your cruelty can make them feel marginalized, reduce intimacy levels between you and cause more harm. Therefore, without dumping your guilt on them: sort things together to continue your friendship.

As children, caretakers should teach us how to maintain good morals. However, trying to do so through punishment can be detrimental because they bank on your guilt response. Our guilt response could have been over-activated for those who received scolding as children, which is now useless in our adult life and makes us feel guilty over usual stuff, like after taking fatty meals or minor inconveniences to others. Instead of guilt or blame, we need to cultivate sound principles by staying open to learning how to be better.

Needless guilt can work against you and stop you from developing into your best self. It can prevent you from changing your behavior because you may feel like admitting that you were involved in something you now consider unethical changes your entire identity and dissociates you from yourself.

Contrary acknowledging your wrongs should give you eagerness to learn humane ways of living instead of triggering shame or guilt.

I envision a world where we may regret our actions and wish to behave differently but refrain from judging ourselves as bad for making mistakes when we don't know better. And feel free to openly critique one another for usual blunders and say, "hey, you were wrong," without suggesting anything is wrong with you.

It would be best if you reconsider how you perceive guilt. Ask yourself, *"How can I stop hurting others and myself in the future?"* Try interrupting your default reactions by realizing that the blame is neither helpful to you nor anyone else. Contemplate doing good more often than punishing yourself and wasting your energy on negative actions.

Think about it;

When last did your behavior hurt someone or yourself?

Did you offer apologies? Did you say something like, "Well, I didn't mean to do that"?

That brings us to:

Do Intentions Matter? If Yours Are Good, Does It Mean Your Behavior Is Excusable?

When the time finally comes for us to take responsibility or apologize for our negative behavior, we could find ourselves saying, "It was never my intention to..." "I didn't mean to hurt you."

Truly, sometimes we do things that hurt others without meaning to.

If you hurt someone unknowingly, and when they let you know, you are saddened and sincerely apologetic, you are probably a genuinely good person who unintentionally hurt someone. It means that although the outcome was terrible and hurtful, it was not your primary intention.

Examples of good intentions gone bad

I recently threw myself into my bed, and as I did so, I elbowed my partner's forehead, causing a lot of pain. I intended to slip into bed as fast as possible to watch a show on Netflix. My partner's head was collateral damage. Of course, I should have been a little more careful, but I wasn't. However, I didn't mean to hurt them.

Another example: say you're debating or arguing with someone over a sensitive topic (like religion). One way or the other, you tell the one with whom you are arguing relevant points that end up hurting them unintentionally.

You were simply pointing out the truth or current religious trends but, in the process, hurt their feelings. Hence, you would say, "I didn't mean to hurt you." It's because you were technically debating with the person and had no intentions of saying anything wrong, although you should have thought twice.

Some of us may use "original intent" to defend ourselves, avoid being accountable, or deny our faults. Coworkers, friends, and even strangers, who bring up intent while apologizing, may try to avoid committing to correct their behavior. Worse, they may redirect the anger toward the one hurting altogether.

You, therefore, should watch out for such apologies. Ask yourself, does the intent of my action truly matter ultimately when the harm has occurred? If you hurt others on purpose or by accident, isn't the outcome the same, regardless of your original intent?

Yes, none of us is immune to error. However, it's essential to know those good intentions aren't excuses for hurtful actions. Upon learning and understanding that, you can effortlessly navigate situations where others want to exploit you (or vice versa), although they "didn't mean to."

However, as long as you are willing to admit that you put your own needs above others in the heat of the moment, it shows some goodness in you. Showing genuine responsibility gives the hurt person the right to be angry rather than expecting forgiveness because you "didn't mean to hurt them." It is immaterial that you didn't mean to; you still hurt them. So, you're accountable for the pain caused.

Also, remember that:

Most problems are fixable. So most likely, it is not as bad as it seems.

Yes, you may be embarrassed and don't feel like forgiving yourself for what you said, did, or didn't do. Maybe you cheated, and your partner found out and divorced you, lied to a friend and hurt their feelings, fought a coworker, or didn't attend a strategic meeting with your boss and got fired. Maybe you feel guilty for missing a workout, overeating despite your weight loss goals, or lazing the entire day and not accomplishing your tasks. All these can make you feel like you have committed the crime of the century, and things will never be the same.

I am here to tell you that even though you feel so bad right now, especially when you think about how much pain you have brought others and yourself, remember it's never that bad. It's all about being human, and we all feel messed up. How you handled the situation may not have been the best way, but that's okay. You are worthy of forgiveness. If everybody had it all figured out, would life be so exciting?

Moreover, dwelling on your past mistakes and beating yourself up won't help anyone at this point. What you need right now is to put yourself together and face the damage you have already caused. We have enough pressure from society; why add to it?

Take a minute and think about your good or bad experiences. What made them different? The most significant difference was whether you were willing or equipped to solve your problem.

For instance...

Some years back, I booked an expedition online with several stopovers, but about eight hours before the trip, I realized that I had made a mistake with one of the stopovers and needed to rectify it. Instead of sitting there and engaging in self-blame and guilt, I called the airline to help me find a solution. It took some time, but they resolved the problem in a way the airline and I were happy about.

You may think you messed up and don't have any strength or skills left to handle this, but remember, life is truly a journey. And just like the most extended road trip would involve some wrong turns, so does your life. You may not know how to handle your blunders, but if you have the belief and desire, you can resolve them. See those mistakes as opportunities: They help you see the areas you should work on to become a better version of yourself.

Here are some ideas to help you get out of a lousy state and see things clearly;

- Take a giant step back from your current situation.

- Get your mind off your current thoughts and emotions.

- Assume you are an observer of the situation, not the participant.

Instead of recreating the bad experience, try to recollect everything that happened like an observer. Rather than saying, "Why do I feel bad I lied?" Try to see it from their perspectives "Why did Kim feel bad I lied? Or instead of

"Why did I get fired? Ask yourself, "Why did my boss fire me?"

Exploring your past mistakes this way somehow changes perspectives and lessens the impact of hurtful emotions. It can display your problems in a larger context and put you in a problem-solving mode. You may think it's weird at first, but it works (as reports by [psychologists](#) suggest)

Luckily for us, most of our mistakes are not essentially life-threatening. Sure, you may end up bruising an ego or lowering your confidence, but there is nothing far beyond repair. Just watch out for how you think after messing up.

Remember two key points when you err:

A mistake doesn't define you unless you let it. When things go wrong, we often don't assume our role as problem solvers— how to reorganize, know what is working or not, how you can improve your state of mind, mend broken ties, forgive yourself, etc. Instead, we mostly feel helpless as victims. But a mistake is an action that doesn't define who you are as a person – only if you let it.

Know there is always a way out. Of course, it does seem like things will ever get better, but you can get out of this situation. After all, you see where the reminiscing of past behavior is taking you. Maybe you have lost many friends or jobs, alienated yourself from caring family members, or become addicted to alcohol trying to soothe your nerves. Don't despair; you are going to be okay. As long as you believe your problems are solvable and are willing to go the extra mile to find solutions, the hell you are going through right now will be over.

You may disapprove, but every issue has a solution. Logical problems, like mathematical problems, may have definite answers, but what about intangible problems like guilt or shame? What about "people's problems"? Although they may lack a "correct" answer, they have a "best" answer, and you need to realize what that is for you.

You could be capable of solving your problem, but are you willing? Maybe you have lost your drive, passion, and motivation due to all the negativity you feel. I get it. As we saw, navigating negative emotions is complex and may require extra effort, determination, and self-sacrifice because it forces you to put yourself first and do something for yourself; this once.

Try to examine your emotions, find possible solutions, and see what happens. You could make a big difference when you take ownership of your life and do not leave your issues to someone else.

Here are a few ways you can become more effective at identifying your mistakes;

Find out what is wrong with your behavior.

Before solving your problems, you need to understand the real issue behind what you feel. Too often, we quickly jump to solutions before fully understanding the problem, so we solve the wrong problem or have mixed results.

For instance, if you cheated, what makes you feel so bad? How did your partner say it made them feel? Are you guilty of cheating, lying, getting caught, or both of these?

That's why you first must do some self-reflection or introspection.

Please use the ideas we discussed earlier to find the natural causes of your problems. Dig into your behavior, look for any symptoms and try to discover the reasons behind it.

Ask yourself questions, gather facts and data, and ensure you step back a little from yourself and adequately understand the situation. Once you have enough information, you can move to the next step.

Picture the outcome you desire

Of course, you want to fix the negative outcome of your emotions. You also expect many positive results, like being happy, etc. What else do you want; to patch things up, get your job back, or cut ties and move on with your life? Write this down.

You cannot solve a problem when unsure of the desired outcome. What outcome would make you happy? What are you looking for that would be a win-win for you and those hurt? Sometimes the desired result is unclear, and you must dig deep to find it. You may need to do more research. This step may seem obvious, but you should not skip it.

Of course, you could be aware of your mistakes but miss some details by jumping straight to the solutions.

The solution lies in the gap

Once you understand your current and expected results, you will see the gap. You can now start addressing it, knowing that you have captured the real issue with the hope of getting the best solution. Indeed, making the right decisions at this point is not always straightforward, but you can do this with more confidence.

With these concepts in mind, don't run from the problem. Tackle it head-on, forge the way forward and enjoy the experience.

Trying to solve problems you caused is what absolves guilt.

In attempting to resolve your wrong behavior, you somehow absolve yourself (sets you free from consequences) of the guilt or shame associated with them.

For example, you realize that you were wrong to cheat on your partner because of how guilty you feel or how bad it hurts your spouse. So you try to fix your improper behavior by apologizing. This somehow absolves you from the guilt of going against your vows. It could clear the air and make you feel better.

Once you identify the mistake, you will see the damage caused by your negative behavior toward yourself and others, understand the pain, and then try to find a solution (e.g., reading this book). And this is more gratifying.

When things go awry in life, we mostly choose to surrender any possible resolutions and choose to wallow in guilt forever. But if we decide to solve our problems and correct our errors, we find ways to live free from the negativity of hurting others and feel content.

What Next?

After establishing how we were responsible for causing the harm or how we could have avoided the problem and mapping out the solution, your first step to absolving guilt is to seek self-atonement.

Forgive yourself!

Three Strategies for Forgiving Yourself When You Know You're in The Wrong

Disconnect your identity from your mistakes

If I'm sincere, I've made mistakes in life, and I haven't always done everything correctly or made the best decisions. The problem was that I used to associate those mistakes with my identity as if I weren't enough or inherently flawed. But the truth is that mistakes do not define you as well as anyone.

Detach yourself from your mistakes. You need to disentangle yourself and see yourself beyond your mistakes. So you knew you erred, accepted it, and then sought forgiveness.

But forgetting is one thing; separating yourself from your mistakes and moving on is another. Clinging to your mistakes keeps you in bondage and stops you from moving on. By moving on, you may feel like you're wearing a mask to hide your nasty side.

At 2. AM after midnight, you may be lying in bed still thinking you are two-faced— pretending you are a good person. Besides, the mistakes will still be there, even with all the time you spent trying to repay them.

I sometimes dug up past mistakes because I felt guilty about leaving them. I could feel guilty for enjoying my life.

Remember that your faults don't essentially define you. Also, you are not your failures. Yes, they are in you, but not you. You are so much more than your mistakes or failures.

You are neither your mistakes nor your failures. Many of us go through life thinking so.

Mistakes are often overwhelming because our brains hang on to them as a constant warning sign. So, your brain could have used the accompanying guilt to ensure you always remember that you're capable of hurting others and prevent you from ever doing it again.

At this point, it is enough. You can stop obsessing over your past mistakes. And chances are you have learned your lesson by now, so the guilt has served its purpose. But it was not supposed to torment you forever.

What happened doesn't define who you are! It could be hard to forget, but you have to. Instead of fearing you'll slip up again, take your lessons and say, "I learned my lesson and will never do that again.

Record your thoughts and feelings

Journaling is an effective healing tool and can benefit your journey to self-forgiveness. Most of us seek recovery at rock bottom when addiction, mental illness, and negativity have eroded our self-worth, confidence, self-image, and self-esteem, among other things. We may have a bucket list of harms we committed against others and a more extensive list of those who played us dirty.

When dealing with negative feelings, I suggest writing down your feelings and finding clear proof. Like you'd handle any list, you need to uncheck things one at a time.

For example, you can write something like, "I lied" or "*I am a liar*." Ask yourself: What did you do that is untrustworthy? Look at it clearly and seek an explanation in the light of other influences." Is it true?

Like you'd handle any list, you need to uncheck the falsities one at a time. Explore your response in writing, perhaps, list the deceitful things you've said or done. It will mostly be a list of most things you are yet to forgive yourself for. Once you see that there is no proof that you are essentially flawed, giving yourself kindness for your mistake becomes easier.

Since it still bothers you years later, you are a trustworthy person engrossed in a lousy situation that maybe you haven't forgiven yourself or asked those you hurt to pardon you.

Ask for forgiveness

Don't forgive for the sake of it. Forgive to receive healing.

First, forgive yourself for hurting yourself because you can't ask others for forgiveness when you still hold grudges against yourself. That will not work.

Therefore, say:

Today, I forgive myself for not sleeping enough, causing my anxiety and bad tempers to escalate. Today, I forgive myself for assuming too many tasks and frequently feel like quitting. And today, I forgive myself for castigating myself when things don't go my way.

If those who love us always forgive us for messing up, we are worthy of forgiveness. We are worthy of being the one who loves ourselves when we don't do our best, and we can comfort ourselves instead of criticizing or judging.

Give yourself a break now. You've tried your best. And I can assure you that it is more than enough. So if you messed up and tore yourself apart, it's okay, but remember that you deserve to forgive yourself and continue to live the beautiful life bestowed.

While at it, remember to ask yourself for forgiveness for;

- All the horrible things you told yourself
- The many times you let yourself down
- Questioning your integrity and character
- Not trusting your first instincts
- Failing to honor your new year's resolutions a thousand times
- Gaining too much weight due to overindulgence
- Not listening to your parents and making the wrong choices as a teenager
- Dropping out of school to be married to the love of your life who later left you
- For all the failed marriages and relationships
- Botched surgeries that embarrass you

- Drinking your way through college and failing exams

- And any other thing that always rings at the back of your head

Secondly, ask others to forgive you for hurting them if you haven't already. As for seeking others' forgiveness, you only need to give a sincere apology. Of course, the one hurt (if alive) needs to know that you have recognized that your behavior was way out of line and you are sorry for that.

Accepting your vulnerability and speaking up is the only way to feel whole again. So for all the horrible things you did to others, the first step is to confess it and own your role in whatever happened. Face or call your team, family, or company. And then ask for forgiveness. Say, "I am sorry for...."

Remember that you don't have to get a hug, be forgiven, or have happy endings. It is only a chance for you to honestly own up to hurting others, seek restoration and righteousness, and set yourself free.

And don't trouble your mind with thoughts on whether the other person will forgive you or not. That's not yours to worry about—do your part!

Everybody is entitled to feel and do however they like, and you have the liberty to discontinue the self-torturing. In other words, if the person does not want to forgive you, that's alright. It is enough that you realize you were wrong, and now you have poured your heart out and let them know how you genuinely feel about your past behavior towards them. What they choose to do with that information should not stop them from letting the negativity go and atoning themselves.

Accept any consequences that follow your apology. Forgiving yourself implies that you also understand that you deserve the result of your actions and that the punishment doesn't have to weigh you down forever.

You could lose your job after confessing to a lie you told your boss. But, be willing to separate yourself from the consequences of your actions.

If you get fired, don't equate the consequences of lying to your identity—avoid labeling yourself as a liar. It does not mean you are a habitual liar. You may have lied to your boss a single time (but just because you forgave yourself did not make it right).

To overcome recurrent guilt, you have to lay out a vision for how to incorporate your lessons into your future actions to ensure that you don't keep repeating the same mistake. Take any consequences you stand to face as turning a new leaf —a chance to start afresh. Think of it as a representation of who you were vs. who you are in the future.

Let's move on to the next chapter.

Chapter 4: Why It Is Moral to Forgive Yourself

Before we consider why it is moral to forgive ourselves, let us first understand what morality means. Morality is our ability to discern right from wrong behavior. By practicing self-forgiveness, we demonstrate our good morals.

How?

To get to the point of self-forgiveness, you must first accept your wrong behavior, atone for it, and then forgive yourself. We recognize when we are bad for hurting others, desire to do the right thing by them, and then forgive ourselves. So, by self-forgiveness, we are doing something morally sound.

Why It Is Compassionate to Forgive Yourself

Compassion is when you notice and get concerned about another's suffering (like when you see a homeless person) and feel so touched by their suffering such that your heart feels their pain ("suffer with") and have the need to show them kindness, care, and offer your help.

Compassion is, therefore, not mere pity; it's more like developing an awareness of others' sufferings, frustrations, and imperfections to help them overcome their misery.

Practicing self-forgiveness is compassionate because it enables you to notice your immense suffering and that of others. You then feel so emphatic about it and want to make things right.

Forgiving yourself makes you aware of the emotional pain of hurting others and gives you a strong desire to stop the pain and self-condemnation, make peace with any past trauma or abuse, and let go of any resentment— all being compassionate acts.

You choose to offer self-kindness over meanness after making mistakes. Instead of mercilessly criticizing yourself for your countless shortcomings or inadequacies, you allow yourself to cultivate understanding and compassion for personal failings – after all, you are not perfect.

Self-forgiveness also shows you care for yourself while understanding that you are still entirely responsible for your actions. It doesn't mean you justify your behavior; instead, you are being compassionate by choosing to make peace with the fact that you hurt others and are empathetic to their experiences without carrying any residual feelings of guilt or shame.

The introspective methods of self-forgiveness help us work on our problems and appreciate that we face unknown triggers, demons, and issues every day and don't mean to hurt others deliberately— reaching such an understanding is compassionate.

As a result, we practice self-compassion when we forgive ourselves.

Self-forgiveness reminds us to eliminate feelings of self-hatred we may have at times and to strive to see ourselves compassionately and treat ourselves with the same kindness and respect that we would show a friend.

In short, there are three critical components to practicing self-compassion that we also apply to self-forgiveness:

1) Recognize and notice your pain.

2) Respond to suffering with kindness and compassion.

3) Keep in mind that imperfection is a part of the human experience that we all share.

Having more compassion for yourself, especially when you are struggling, can help you maintain a positive attitude toward yourself.

When well utilized, compassion and empathy are practical forgiveness tools.

Indeed, you cannot fully leverage the healing power of forgiveness without accepting and working through your emotions or feelings. And that's why we must nurture empathy and compassion—for others and ourselves. By acknowledging that we are all fallible beings and subject to our life perspectives and experiences, we start seeing ourselves and others with much more understanding.

We say, "Yes, I made mistakes, hurt others, or made bad decisions based on my emotional maturity and experience. Others have also made mistakes based on what they knew at the time." Often, internalizing this fact requires us to set our egos aside and assume another person's perspective, and we should not expect it to happen immediately.

But with more mindfulness, patience, and kindness, over time, you can understand that your actions had little to do with hurting others. You were only reflecting your emotional immaturity.

That said, compassion should not negate boundaries. You can still have a heart for the pain and events that led to hurting others and still choose to block toxic people from your life and stop them from triggering the worst in you. Moreover, having compassion or empathy for yourself does not give you a pass for lousy behavior. Yet, withholding forgiveness or kindness to punish yourself for hurting yourself or others will only show more toxic hatred in your energy. As we mentioned, this toxicity can manifest in your words and deeds.

Why It Is Fair to Forgive Yourself

We often hear children say, "That's not fair," but what does this entail? Fairness is treating everyone equally and making just decisions (considering pros and cons) without exploiting anyone. It also involves sharing stuff equally and only having your fair share. Being honest also means avoiding unjustly or carelessly blaming people.

How is forgiving yourself fair?

Why do we tend to quickly forgive others' wrongdoing and not forgive ourselves when we go wrong? It is only fair to give ourselves what we would give others— forgiveness.

As I have defined fairness, you can see that by embracing self-forgiveness, you make a rational decision to free yourself from any mental bias and injustices against you or others and choose to face your problems impartially. You decide not to blame yourself for the things that are not your fault but admit to your weaknesses, and that's fair enough.

As you know, blaming oneself and guilt is a one-sided approach to problems. But changing your mind, taking your fair share of the mistakes, and saying, "I was wrong for this and that. Please forgive me, " creates room for negotiation, allowing the aggrieved party and the wrongdoer to come to the table and work on arriving at an amicable solution together.

Moreover, letting go of all past mistakes makes room for a fair playing ground when dealing with others. At least you are no longer weighed down by emotional burdens.

Self-forgiveness gives you a chance to go outside the box, assume a reasonable way to look at things that enables you to perceive other people's hurts, and grasp precisely how you are responsible for causing them. Through practicing self-forgiveness, you establish that we all have inner struggles, and nobody is immune to mistakes. Hence, it's only fair to stop beating yourself up when you make mistakes and show yourself kindness like you would another person.

Once you realize none of us is perfect, you stop labeling others as good or bad or vice versa.

Why It Is Empowering to Forgive Yourself

Betrayals, arguments, and mistakes can disrupt our happiness by increasing stress and destroying our mental and physical health. As challenging as it might seem, forgiveness empowers you to face these problems with a kind heart and let them go. Therefore it frees you from the emotions that hinder you from having inner peace. Self-forgiveness makes you feel empowered to proceed positively.

As illustrated, past triggers often fuel our insecurities and leak out unresolved pain. Listing all your triggers and letting them go one by one can help you free yourself from the fear, anger, and anxiety that are holding you back. By identifying your triggers and figuring out your hindrances, you achieve autonomy over them, take back your control, and get ready to tackle them when they present themselves.

As I said, most people you hurt may have moved on or passed on and are not here to engage with, but you still need to speak your truth. Using honesty and empathically expressing your pain re-establishes your boundaries from the pain and empowers you to overcome your problems.

Self-forgiveness helps you review your expectations and sets realistic ones, which empowers your future relationships with others. You accept that you will often let yourself and others down in one way or another, so it's unrealistic to assume you will be perfect after you forgive yourself. Accepting that you will not always see eye to eye with everyone, you can agree to disagree and keep going. Moreover, since you know the ones you hurt don't have to forgive you, you can manage your expectations and appreciate your small wins.

By ending the self-blame and guilt, you take control of your life. Instead of letting every action, word, or mistake trigger you, face everything empathetically and compassionately. You feel empowered to forge the best way forward with much respect and love. If, for instance, you have marital problems, you can decide to walk away from the toxicity or start afresh with the same person.

Why It Is Loving to Forgive Yourself

We have heard many songs and poems about love, but we often mistake it for a whirlwind feeling of romance. But what does love encompass? Love is that profoundly warm, passionate affection for others; as for a child, parent, or friend, it is a sense of deep attachment or affection.

So what does self-love entail? We consider it the most basic human emotion, yet we don't understand love. But for the sake of self, we will talk about self-love because it is one of the vital ingredients in forgiving yourself when everything seems messed up. By forgiving yourself, you cultivate self-love.

Self-love is having a significant concern for your happiness and well-being. Self-love implies caring for your needs without sacrificing others' well-being and comfort. Self-love is appreciating oneself with actions supporting your physical, mental, and spiritual evolution. It means you choose not to settle for anything below your values or standards.

Self-love enables you to accept your emotional state and place your emotional, physical, and mental health first. It prefers showing yourself love over hate. Therefore, forgiveness is a healing type of self-love. Like everything worth acquiring and attaining, self-forgiveness takes a lot of self-love. It may be hard to do, yet you are guaranteed to have the most incredible sense of love, peace, and acceptance once you attain self-love.

Forgiving yourself is loving because it allows you to;

- Approach yourself with a lot of love even when you feel underserved.

- Prioritize yourself and seek your healing first.

- Trust yourself enough to know that you always do your best under the circumstances.

- Stop self-judgment and instead embrace understanding.

- Be friendly to yourself and not think that you are a terrible person for erring.

- Stay true to yourself; accept responsibility for a wrong and not blame yourself unfairly.

- Set firm boundaries for those who instill guilt in you unnecessarily.

- Forgive yourself for everything.

- Be kind to yourself and others even when things go wrong.

All these are tenets of self-love.

Self-forgiveness can stop you from acting against others due to unhealed pain in yourselves. Any negative energy you have in yourself is released rather than cast onto everyone near you, which is a loving way to treat others.

In short, the call for self-forgiveness is an opportunity to discover more about yourself, evolve beyond your ego's desire, and start living from the heart.

Why The World Wants You to Forgive Yourself

We can fuel negative emotions to sustain them over a long period as a reminder that we messed up and deserve to feel the pain. For instance, having vengeful thoughts about an event you dislike only intensifies your feelings about the experience.

As we mentioned, some people don't respond with compassion toward a suffering person, especially when they feel the person deserves punishment. And several studies show that the desire for revenge is sometimes stronger than empathy, especially in men. A moment of anger could therefore wipe out a lifetime of good.

The empathy cultivated through self-forgiveness can help us connect to the rest of humanity by seeing the situation from a different perspective and attempting to understand what could have contributed to the behavior that triggered the harm.

It can result in a change in attitudes about ourselves and others. So many psychologists suggest that if we learn how to forgive ourselves earlier, the mental disorders that arise in some people (serial killers, rapists, or psychos) due to pent-up anger, guilt, or shame may be easier to resolve.

In addition, cultivating self-forgiveness is essential because many people commit senseless crimes in a fit of anger. As shown earlier, some acts of violence happen out of ignorance or carelessness, but circumstances prompt others. They can occur outside our control, especially when our emotional and mental conditions are unhealthy. However, one fleeting moment of anger can cause serious crimes that can change our lives forever and make it difficult to forgive, thus fueling more hate and resentment in the world.

Through self-forgiveness, we identify and overcome such dangerous emotions and increase the chances of neutralizing resentment and freeing us from its grip. By giving us a better way to deal with such feelings, helping us see things differently, and rediscovering our positive qualities. Adverse events can become opportunities to positively reframe our minds, resolve conflicts better, and maintain world peace.

As we generate more compassion and empathy through self-forgiveness, we can feel connected to the experience of all those in pain and do something to help them. We can develop tolerance and patience, appreciate the complexity of our human condition, cultivate mindfulness, wisdom, giving, generosity, and honesty among members of society and bring an end to world suffering.

If we practiced self-forgiveness globally, we would have fewer diseases to deal with, reducing our global health budget significantly. We would then use the spared resources to provide food for the hungry and help the poor and less fortunate.

Happier, healthier individuals, therefore, create a better world.

Now that you have learned the moral aspects of self-forgiveness let us look at some of its social aspects.

Chapter 5: Why It Is Socially Responsible to Forgive Yourself

We are all responsible for acting to benefit society, not solely ourselves, and should work in our environment's and society's best interests. Therefore practicing self-forgiveness is good for society because it can help us realize when we hurt others and stop us from causing more harm.

Society Benefits When You Forgive Yourself

Here are a few ways forgiveness is good for society;

Self-forgiveness nurtures relationships

Self-forgiveness allows you to overcome pain, guilt, and anger, plus reconcile and restore damaged relationships. It is a process that encourages general acceptance and helps us change our destructive behavior and attitudes to create constructive relationships and sustainable peace. Some transgressions can potentially limit personal and interpersonal relationships if we fail to forgive ourselves.

For instance, as children and teenagers, we may have hurt people with our ignorant behavior because we were still in the learning phase and fighting with raging hormones.

Moreover, we still had self-esteem issues and were prone to social anxiety because of our fragile immature egos.

Sometimes we may have felt so guilty, ashamed, and hated ourselves for hurting our caregivers, not following their instructions, and making a mess. The 'I told you so' could make us feel so bad. And even long after apologizing, we still beat ourselves up for letting others down. Such strong emotions can overwhelm a young person to the point of committing suicide or running away.

Practicing self-forgiveness can come in handy for such teenagers by helping them eliminate any hate, guilt, or shame they feel for misbehaving and hurting others, putting their past behind them, and moving on. They can become more loving, understanding, and compassionate towards themselves and others, thereby creating more balanced, meaningful relationships and becoming less harmful to others in society. So self-forgiveness (when taught earlier) can help us learn to be more about ourselves and build happier communities.

Forgiveness can transform general attitudes

"If you want to change others, you must first change yourself."

Our initial attitudes about ourselves when we make mistakes may be damaging. We usually perceive ourselves as horrible and blame ourselves for going against our values or wrongdoings. But once we start working on forgiveness, we change our attitudes about ourselves and our behavior. We decide to look at things differently, away from our initial standpoint.

Practicing self-forgiveness helps us acknowledge the possibility of each other's susceptibility to err, stop seeing ourselves as enemies and start appreciating our uniqueness. We soften our hard stands, change our attitudes, become more accountable, reconcile and even help to transform other people's perceptions, attitudes, and prejudices by mirroring our behavior.

Such noble actions can set an excellent example for others and inspire them to be more forgiving. Our self-forgiveness can also help transform other people's perceptions, attitudes, and prejudices as they mirror our behavior. For instance, when perpetrators practice self-forgiveness, they can change their attitudes, make amends and prepare to re-enter society as free better beings.

In this situation, self-forgiveness can enable the perpetrators to willingly start anew and open themselves to becoming peaceful, productive community members. And when the victims practice self-forgiveness, they can let go of their pain and resentment and probably even allow their perpetrator to compensate for their wrongdoing, setting an excellent example for others.

Even criminals can exercise self-forgiveness while in jail. After the relevant authorities approve that they have changed, they can be given parole and return to a more tolerant society willing to take them back and not discriminate against them based on their past. The repentant persons can get jobs, marry and become good citizens.

Imagine a society where we are free to be ourselves, willing to own up to mistakes, make amends, let go of the guilt and shame, and forgive ourselves for all the wrongs done to others and ourselves. Punitive justice (police, judges, and jails) will be less necessary in such cases because people would be more accountable for their mistakes and apologize. And it would be hard for anyone to repeat an offense after the entire self-forgiveness process.

Self-forgiveness encourages helping needy society members.

We discover that we all struggle with different things through the increased awareness triggered by self-forgiveness. And, as we become more empathetic and compassionate, we notice some of us are immensely suffering, so helping others becomes our social duty.

Once we know how our actions affect others, we can guard our behavior closely not to hurt others and become more involved in resolving societal problems. We can be inspired to start giving back to society by donating our time, assets, or money to the community, for instance:

- Engaging in charitable acts, like philanthropy, financial donations, etc.

- Assisting the needy community by volunteering, working at an animal shelter, elderly homes, or food bank, or giving blood donations.

- Advocating issues affecting us and the general public politically or socially—for example, ending child labor, promoting fair laws, trade, and recycling.

- Upholding personal ethics, such as honesty and integrity. Following the "golden rule" of treating others like you want them to treat you—with love, compassion, empathy, fairness, and forgiveness.

Friends and Family Benefit When You Forgive Yourself

Most of our families aren't perfect. Sometimes we can say or do despicable things to our loved ones and feel guilty for "sinning" toward them. Self-forgiveness helps us rebuild solid, healthy relationships with our family members by helping us navigate the issues that hurt the relationship in the first place. It helps clarify the situation and allows us to see who or what went wrong.

Accepting your mistake and apologizing for your part in the wrong can help resolve any resentment your loved ones feel towards you and enables you to find ways to mend the relationship together.

Besides helping you heal from past childhood trauma, practicing self-forgiveness can also help you understand why your family mistreated or abused you as a child.

Suppose you were punished unfairly by your parents or older siblings for minor mistakes. During your moments of reflection and research, you could discover that those relatives who mistreated you could have also experienced lousy parenting or suffered atrocities in their childhood and were only projecting their pain onto you unknowingly.

Moreover, if a family member sexually molested you as a child or teenager, practicing self-forgiveness can help you eliminate the 'it's my fault syndrome' with daily affirmations and extra self-love. Once you work through the unhealthy guilt and establish that you are not at fault for being abused, you can eventually gain the courage to face your offender and ask questions. After talking to them, you could decide to forgive them because you now come from a place of understanding, compassion, and love.

By learning that various factors can make us unintentionally hurt others, you let go of the self-hatred and negative criticism that consumes you. You can stop blaming yourself or others for what went wrong. And once you 'let things go,' you can get past the offense, move on with your life, and choose to start afresh. And make new friends or try to revive old friendships or romance.

Additionally, as you reflect on your inappropriate behavior and seek forgiveness, you can mend broken family ties if desired. While reaching out to relatives and old friends, you prepare for any response they give you. You know they may accept your apology but want nothing to do with you, and that's fine. However, you also know that if your old-timers reject your apologies, you have a higher chance of making new friends and strengthening your current and future family bonds in your positive emotional state.

Everybody can enjoy hanging out with this friendlier, loving new you who is a better friend, mother, father, sister, or child to your parents. Expressing regret and correcting the behavior that intentionally or unintentionally hurt others is a critical step toward self-forgiveness that helps restore relationships. Feeling guilty motivates us to fix the observed wrongs or try to "right the wrong."

So, as long as we have done everything we can to directly express our regret to the other person, even if they are not receptive to our efforts to reach out, it somehow helps with closure. And as you gain closure, you open the door for more understanding within your family unit and circle of friends, and soon you may be closer than before and could even forget why you parted ways. And as you nurture more love and compassion in your relationships, you build stronger bonds and can navigate disagreements easier.

The Future Becomes Better When You Forgive Yourself

Forgiving yourself empowers you to tackle future family problems free from guilt or shame. You can be free to express yourself without judgment, guilt, or shame, but if you hurt anyone in the process, you choose to apologize and go on with life agreeably. In turn, you build stronger, healthier family bonds and friendships.

According to research, punishing ourselves for our mistakes is harmful because it makes us feel hopeless and stuck in self-doubt. Engaging in self-forgiveness helps you to stop punishing yourself too much for transgressions and become more confident to face future relationship problems. It also allows you to gradually release negative feelings while restoring positive emotions like respect and love, which are good foundations for happy relationships.

In business or at work, practicing self-forgiveness helps you learn to handle your future failure and mistakes with grace and compassion. When you realize that some losses are not your fault, you can halt the self-blame or guilt from failed projects or job loss. You understand external factors could interfere with your work, and there is nothing you can do to change that. Accepting the inevitability of bad things happening without your interference makes you confident to face your future work-related problems.

As a boss who has practiced self-forgiveness, your increased self-awareness, emotional resilience, compassion, and empathy can help you handle prospective employees from the point of love and understanding. You will not scold, criticize or punish errant workers without factoring in other issues that could make them come to work late, lie to you, steal, fight with fellow staff, or do any other wrong things. You start looking at work issues from different perspectives, put yourself in your employee's shoes, and experience what they go through.

You can notice if they are understaffed, underpaid, sick, hurt, overworking, and any other problem they may be going through and do something to help. You also make sound, quick decisions no longer clouded by negativity from your past trauma or experiences. In short, having dealt with your self-loathing and pain, you can become a better future employer or boss, in tune with employees who could, in turn, improve their performance and overall business performance.

Employers appreciate an emotionally stable, honest, happy, and confident employee. Practicing self-forgiveness can help you become a better employee when you see your wrongs and own up to your error instead of keeping others guessing who did this or that. You would also want to do better next time.

Most bosses can show leniency even for the worst mistake if you come clean, apologize, and act accordingly. You could avoid getting fired or resume work if your boss has already fired you. And if you keep your behavior that good, you could even get a promotion when your boss notices. You may even change jobs swiftly and secure better-paid jobs. So, with your improved self, you rest assured of a brighter, rewarding, long career ahead.

You now have the complete picture of how you and everyone stand to gain from self-forgiveness.

Next, let us see how society can make us guilty, ashamed, and anxious without reason.

Chapter 6: How Society Conditions You to Feel Guilt You Do Not Deserve

According to research on human behavior, we form most of our beliefs and behavior during childhood. Our parents, teachers, siblings, and peers influence our thoughts and behavior through their words and actions.

So you may primarily define yourself (who you are) based on how others perceive you during childhood, shaping your social interactions and personal choices.

Your childhood also gave you ideas about people, whether people are inherently good or willing to help others, and whether they hurt each other on purpose.

Moreover, if your childhood was full of love and care, you may have learned that it's okay to trust and help others. If people weren't so kind, you could have held the belief that others could hurt or exploit you.

You would consider the world safe if you grew up in a caring environment with rare adverse events as a child. You may even anticipate living in a positive, peaceful world. However, suppose you have experienced extreme, unpredictable events and endured chronic stress. In that case, you may consider the world scary, and you must struggle to succeed regardless of what you do.

How we react to a stressful situation is mostly an aggregate of what happened in our younger years, and our hard-wired programming influences our coping mechanisms. So, we respond to problems differently, primarily based on our past conditioning and traumatic experiences. The emotional or physical experiences you went through as a child continue to affect your responses, ultimately becoming the coping tools you rely on to protect yourself.

You may have encountered people who try to make you feel guilty or blame you for a mistake, even knowing it's not your fault. It is normal to hear people make hurtful comments about you to make you feel insufficient and guilty for things you did not do or did by mistake. And since there are plenty of such kinds of people, this happens on a societal level. So, let us learn how.

How Society Conditions Undeserved Blame

There are some blatant and subtle ways society can finger-point us into feeling guilty and ashamed for no reason:

Societal expectations

We grew up knowing that there is a specific criterion of things to attain as told by our teachers, priests, parents, movies, TV, friends, and neighbors. From a young age, we had a picture of the ideal weight, height, beauty, behavior, talent, and marriage partner.

We had a perfect career list; doctor, lawyer, dentist, surgeon, pilot, foot-baller, basket-baller, movie star, celebrity, and so on. We learned and accepted that by this or that age, we should have accomplished this or that. And that's alright. However, some careers and standards set by our society may be unattainable for some of us. We may fail to meet or attain some of them for one reason or another or not accomplish them in perfect order.

The following are statements you might have heard, although not necessarily in that order;

"When and where are you going to go to college?"

And if you do graduate college but fail to get a job,

"Why are you not trying to get a job?"

And if you do get a job,

"When are you going to get married or marry, and you are getting older?"

And when you get married but don't have children a few years down,

"Is it not the time for you to have a child?"

And if you do get one,

"When will you give _____ someone to play with? Or give us a boy this time?"

And when you gain weight from childbirth or whatnot,

"When are you hitting the gym? You are becoming heavy."

And so on!

As highlighted in the statements above, society expects us to be of a certain weight, skin color, and height, finish school at a certain age, start working and become financially stable at a certain age, get married at a certain age, and eventually sire children. These milestones are all good when attained. But what if things don't work out this way?

What if you drop out of school due to lack of school fees, don't get As or scholarships needed for college admission, don't get a job due to an economic crisis, don't get married or get divorced for some reason, or cannot have children because biology doesn't allow it? Society then judges you harshly, discriminates, blames, and makes you feel guilty for things you cannot control and, therefore, are not your fault.

People discriminate and point fingers at you for failing to meet general societal expectations. They can pressure you and make you do everything to get yourself out of your situation.

We can even take extreme measures (like life-threatening surgeries) to correct your problem, but it could be in vain. If you fail to timely graduate with honors, get rich faster, get a baby (or a couple of them), or get employed, they force you to accept that you are a failure because 'so and so did it.' When repeated often enough, you may subconsciously start to believe them and feel guilty and ashamed for not succeeding like everybody else you know.

Those who have—secured employment (it doesn't matter how), succeeded in getting married (could be unhappy), given birth (many times), became rich before 40 (the means don't count), and are probably rich and famous (by whatever means) — are idolized by society. Often, the 'successful' ones look down on the 'not-so-successful' society members like it is their fault for not achieving the set milestones in life.

Their hurtful remarks, insults, threats, or violence are oppressive behavior. Racism, sexism (gender bias), religious persecution, and economic oppression (mistreatment based on income) are all forms of social oppression (unfairly treating people who are different from you).

Of course, we should do our best to succeed in the goals we set for ourselves. But the truth is that some of our childhood fantasies we may not attain. And, in reality, we will make many mistakes—some we will pull through, some we won't. Of course, it can be depressing to see your 'successful' friends on Facebook and Instagram uploading cute babies, showing off their master's degrees, fancy cars, and handsome or wealthy husbands— when you feel pretty stuck in life.

However, if you make a mistake and don't accomplish some of these milestones, it is unfair to hide your face or let others' criticism, accusations, and intimidation get the best of you. You could end up depressed by this superficial shame and guilt.

I emphasized self-forgiveness for blaming and criticizing yourself unfairly. It will help you appreciate yourself for the far you have come, do your best to salvage what's left of your life, and focus on becoming your best. You could even start a career, discover a hidden talent that puts you on the wealthiest or most famous list or get a baby or mate at 40 and beyond. Remember that we are all different, and so be you!

Culture

Culture is our way of life; it entails beliefs, arts, and an institution passed down from one generation to another and affects an entire society. It contains codes of manners, language, dress, religion, art, and rituals. Our culture plays a role; it can shape how we behave and affect how we perceive ourselves and others. It also influences our values—the interpretation of right from wrong. Although following a particular culture can give you a sense of belonging and acceptance, it could be a stumbling block to self-forgiveness.

Some cultures, for example, have stringent rules about sex; however, Australian culture has a casual approach to sex. If someone grows up in Australia, but their parents are from a different culture, they might feel guilty about their sexual behavior because of the inharmonious value systems.

So there are subtle ways society makes us feel guilty or ashamed for a particular behavior. It may be to uphold acceptable behavior and encourage responsibility when we hurt others.

However, you may do something culturally wrong to others and hurt their feelings unawares— maybe by how you dress, talk or do things. Once those people criticize you, you could start feeling guilty or ashamed, although you no longer belong to the culture or believe in their norms.

Religion

Another strong influencer that relies on feelings of guilt to show that a person has done something wrong is our religious traditions. Some religious people quickly take offense to people who do or say something ignorant of their beliefs and may scold you unfairly. You may be left feeling guilty and ashamed for being accused of discriminating against the members of the religion.

Also, if you find yourself in a situation that contradicts your religious values and beliefs, you may feel guilty for not simply conforming to the doctrines like everybody else.

For example, as a staunch follower of a specific religion (say Buddhism, Wiccan, Muslim, or Christianity), you may feel bad for going against your religious principles. For instance, the Koran (Surah 4: An-Nisa': 2-3) permits marrying many wives among the Muslim people in specific circumstances; therefore, any Muslim man who rightly practices polygamy would not feel guilty or ashamed of it. However, a single

Muslim woman who does not want to be married as a second wife may be shunned or shamed.

Social pressure

There is a lot of social pressure behind the scenes. Now and then, we face immense invisible pressure to conform to certain societal expectations to avoid the harsh penalties for violating the often unwritten social rules. Many of us are cautious of our behavior and words because we fear transgressing the values and standards set by our society. Suppose someone accuses you of doing or saying something socially unacceptable— for instance, if you fail to support the ideas behind a moral crusade (a social movement that campaigns around a moral or symbolic issue like pornography or alcohol found on Facebook or Instagram). Its members could primarily single you out and condemn you for posting something that contradicts their mostly extremist views.

Being targeted with such hate for simply expressing yourself but in a way that goes against their ideas on morality may make you feel guilty and remorseful for the unfair judgment.

That said...

Tons of Oppressive Institutions Propel Shame

Institutions like courts, schools, media or the military sometimes discriminate against people based on race, gender, income, or religion.

For instance, because of their origin, black people have suffered institutional racism whereby they seem marginalized, powerless, and exploited on various issues concerning their wealth, income, employment, justice, health care, housing, education, and politics.

Many institutions exist for different purposes, including educational, media, legal, health care, government, social service, and criminal justice systems. However, when we talk about oppressive institutions, it is when such laws, practices, and customs seem to favor a particular group of people more than the other.

Their belief that the favored ones are superior produces inequalities in society. It often leads to people's oppression (mistreatment or harassment) solely based on their identity and the groups they belong to now. That can result in abuse, assaults, bullying, and aggression toward people who are said to belong to the 'wrong' group.

Therefore, oppressive institutions indirectly discriminate and curtail members of the 'unfavorable' social identity groups. If we are the target of such oppression, it can leave us feeling guilty or ashamed for belonging to particular groups of people—often not by choice. Sadly, the only people who cannot see the barriers are those NOT directly affected by such forms of cruelties.

We Can't Stop Society, But We Can Protect Ourselves

To reduce the impact of receiving threats, mistreatment, or cruelty because of your ethnicity or race, sexual orientation, religious affiliation, gender identity, country of origin, or any other identity issue, use the following strategies:

Avoid being around the perpetrators

First, to avoid falling prey to other people's cruelty, be responsible for your safety. As this martial arts motto goes, "The ultimate self-defense method is to not put yourself in a situation where you must defend yourself." You can do this by;

Trusting yourself. In most cases, our eyes, skin, nose, ears, and tongue give us clues about impending threats. Our sixth sense could also tip us off. So trust your instincts when they tell you that something(or someone) doesn't seem right.

Stay conscious of your surroundings. Regardless of how safe you think you are when around some people, beware of their behavior towards you and notice when they are being offensive. To tell peoples' intentions, pay attention to them. Notice how the person looks at you or when they make you feel uneasy.

Heed to these forewarnings even when around people you trust because, as we mentioned, the perpetrator could be a close friend, an intimate relative, or an acquaintance. We can prevent needless guilt and shame by constantly examining others' intentions.

Act focused and confident. Often, perpetrators look for people who seem weak, timid, soft, and unfocused. They can quickly spot easy picks— someone they can attack without much resistance. That's why I said you should assert yourself around such people. Make eye contact to warn the would-be transgressor that you are in control and aware of their intention. In the same way, you can tell other people's feelings; they also sense yours.

Second, it's okay to avoid or cut off people who remain disrespectful to you, your values, or your identity, despite warning them to stop their behavior. If you are always around people who are ignorant of your concerns, they will constantly make you feel wrong with their actions and words.

The people we spend our time with have a significant influence on us. When we spend time with friends, family, or coworkers in a bad mood, their attitude can rub off on us. When conversing with someone cynical about the world, constantly complaining about their job, or gossiping about a typical associate, it is easy to fall into less-than-ideal conversational patterns and start feeling more critical of ourselves.

If you notice that you feel bad after spending time with certain people, try to reduce your time with them. Spend less time with that fellow who always wants to argue. Unfriend that person on social media who constantly posts offensive memes.

Alternatively, try to steer your conversations with them toward more positive or neutral topics, and if your attempts to engage them in healthy communication are futile, avoid them altogether. (Note: this does not imply abandoning a friend who is ill.) Give positive relationships more significance in your life. Instead of hanging around toxic people, connect with caring, supportive, and like-minded people. Visit a supportive friend if being with your family is overwhelming for you.

Avoid negative news on tv, in newspapers, or on social media

We are constantly bombarded with harrowing information, nasty debates, and alarmist headlines, causing us to feel traumatized and terrible. As you watch the news, you may feel responsible for the bad news, although you cannot do anything to change the aired situation.

Unfortunately, negativity sells stories.

For instance, suppose you saw two articles —the first headline stated, "The weather is beautiful today!" The second one said that a massive dark storm was heading your way. Which one would you automatically click on?

Almost certainly the second one, because you would like to know how the impending storm could affect your day! That's the approach the media has used for years, which urges viewers to stay tuned to listen to 'real stories about how some things can endanger or affect their lives.

Because we inherently react to threats based on a "negativity bias" (the tendency to be keen on negative details than on positive ones), and like Google, our minds usually highlight weird stuff.

Since the media's inception, it has leveraged negativity to increase profits. Many conflicts and wars have begun based on lies reported by corrupt journalists. Some people use the term "yellow journalism," inferring that the press can sometimes propagate outright lies while presenting them as facts of the day.

While we have algorithms that detect fake news and laws against giving outright provocative false information (hate speech), we can't wholly avoid negative news. The media uses it to attract more viewers and clicks, which means more revenue. Results on Google search also often respond to our unconscious hunger for negativity by giving us what we seemingly want —which usually means more bad news.

Suppose you aren't watchful of such inclination to negativity and continually read negative stuff or watch films or documentaries perpetuating violence and social injustices.

In that case, you may pick harmful content and images that will later trouble your mind. You may also fill your heart with resentment and your mind with guilt for not being able to do anything to help. Therefore it's okay sometimes to shut the

TV off, change the program, and become picky with reading social media posts or newspapers.

Stay positive

To remain positive, you first need to embrace positive thinking.

To help you understand how your thoughts bring about significant changes in your brain function, affecting how you feel, allow me to digress a bit.

For starters, the amygdala (the part of the brain that processes and reacts to negative emotions like anxiety, guilt, depression, or positive emotions like joy) regulates our emotions. When you think positively, it activates the amygdala, making you have positive emotions, and when you think negatively, the alternative happens.

Secondly, thoughts (whether positive or negative) can also affect certain chemicals in our brains. For instance, Cortisol (a stress-inducing hormone) decreases when you have happy thoughts or are feeling joyful. The brain generates serotonin (a feel-good hormone) responding to your positivity. When serotonin levels are stable, one can be more focused, happy, less anxious, calm, and emotionally stable.

The other critical feel-good hormones are endorphins which trigger positive feelings for doing something enjoyable, such as laughing, having sex, or exercising, and dopamine which your brain releases when you do pleasurable things or finish a task.

Positive thinking entails having a more optimistic attitude to life, focusing on the positive instead of negative stuff, and remaining confident rather than discouraged, which positively influences your feel-good hormones and the amygdala. When life brings you challenges, you choose to meet them with a self-reliant, positive attitude.

Also, change negative thought patterns using affirmations or a thought replacement technique to silence your inner critic by countering negative thoughts with positive thoughts every time they arise.

When you notice a negative thought about yourself or others, interrupt it with something positive. For instance, if you're thinking, "I'm so stupid for failing that interview." You can say to yourself, "I'm smart. I went out there and tried my best. Even if I didn't get the job, I'm okay.

More tips for escaping negative thoughts;

Label your thoughts

Instead of judging whether your thoughts are truths or not, label them as they are. Phrase each thought as "I have a thought that is …". Label your thoughts as they are without changing, adapting, or avoiding the original thought.

By labeling your thoughts, you can get some distance between your thoughts and you as a person. You can distinguish whether these thoughts reflect you or are just negative thoughts spiraling out of control.

Notice when you're getting into the mean, negative cycle

Be wary of your negative automatic thought patterns, e.g., your all-or-nothing thinking. This type of thinking prevents us from seeing the situation as it is. Thinking about something as ALWAYS or NEVER:

- Makes us believe that things can't change over time
- Makes it seem like we can predict the future
- Gets us stuck in one of two extremes, both uncomfortable and unrealistic.

What precedes a negative thinking spiral? Be aware of your triggers. Knowing your triggers makes you more likely to notice when you're getting wrapped up in your negative thinking.

Top Tip: Instead of using the words "always," "never," "everyone," or "nothing," use words like "sometimes," "some people," and "often."

Pause

Suppose you notice yourself feeling stressed, anxious, or in a low mood. Acknowledge that you are engaging in these thoughts. Focus instead on your emotions and where you feel them in your body. Pause the thinking and tune into your body sensations to get more grounded.

Lastly, do things that make you happy because when happy, you balance your brain chemicals and ward off negativity easily. During your break from toxicity, do something else to help you relax and revitalize; take a walk, a hot bath, or snack, massage, watch a movie, or do any other fun thing to get your mind off the negativity.

Avoid using alcohol and drugs to "check out" your sad and stressful state. You may feel nice for a moment but not as rejuvenated as doing something socially active and creative. Trying to escape or cope with guilt and shame and using drugs can intensify them because you may start behaving in a way you would never while sober.

Having mentioned how society can make us feel guilty for a few things, it is also essential to understand something else.

Although society has its way of making us feel guilty for things we are not to blame for, we should not always make excuses for our behavior. Not admitting your fault can damage your relationships and delay your personal growth.

Having some pride is okay. It can push you ahead in the presence of challenging situations and give you that self-assuredness everyone aspires for in their professional and personal lives. But a thin line divides positive confidence and a stubborn ego.

One of the leading pointers that you are on the wrong side is failing to accept when you are wrong. Some of us can't admit fault because we have poor self-awareness (a widespread, ongoing issue) or have a "blind spot" in some social situations. In any case, if a person isn't aware they're wrong, then they may have difficulties admitting to wrongdoing.

In some cases, although you may be aware that you're mistaken, you may struggle with waving the guilty flag because of your ego.

As Kate Kaplan, a California psychologist, says, *"admitting a mistake could be scary for some people because it challenges their inflated self-image, making them feel guilty or ashamed and questions their principles or character. People often deny fault or refuse to own their mistakes to protect their self-image."*

Due to a process known as cognitive dissonance (an automatic defense system for protecting our ego), psychologists suggest that some people struggle with admitting fault, knowing they are wrong because of the worry that it exposes their imperfection.

It often makes them feel nasty, weak, or even inherently wrong. Moreover, their intense fears make them always worry about losing respect or destroying a bond. So for them to say, "Indeed, I messed up, I'm sorry," may be terrifying. However, firmly denying our wrongs frustrates our family, colleagues, peers, and partners. Furthermore, it stifles our progress and makes people distance themselves from us and isolate us.

Since the primary cause of refusing to admit our mistakes is our fragile ego, it may become a self-fulfilling prophecy that confirms our inability to be loved when our loved ones push us away. We often avoid vulnerability by denying responsibility to prevent destroying our defense walls.

When we avoid vulnerability, we cling to feelings of guilt, shame, and fear, which can eventually take a toll on our mental health, causing anxiety or depression.

However, admitting flaws lets others see our openness, charms them, and opens doors to meaningful conversations. Conversely, admitting our wrongs shows we are empathetic, compassionate, considerate, and good listeners. Additionally, it can show we are objective and not trying to be 'always right' or 'perfect.'

Taming Your Ego

Here are a few techniques to help you improve at controlling your ego;

Bow into our human condition

Adopt this mantra and repeat it when you cannot admit fault: "I can admit I'm wrong because I am human, and we all make mistakes, and I am lovable despite this."

We will learn more about mantras shortly.

Get introspective

List all your flaws and ask essential reflective questions, such as:

- ☐ "How have my actions impacted others I care about?"
- ☐ "Do I have patience?"
- ☐ "Why am I afraid to be vulnerable?"
- ☐ "What role did I play in a recent argument?"
- ☐ "Do I have anger issues?"
- ☐ "Am I insecure?"
- ☐ "Am I overly jealous?"
- ☐ "Am I selfish?"

Remember that self-reflection is helpful, but rumination is destructive. Brooding over problems, magnifying misfortunes, and hosting a pity party escalate your distress. So, every time you rehash painful times, your confidence drops, hopelessness soars, and guilt intensifies.

Ask for feedback

If it is not easy to take personal accountability for your mistakes, it could be helpful to go to people in your life who are caring, supportive, and eager to help. It may look daunting to appear vulnerable, but remember that it could unearth your much-needed acceptance and profound emotional connection.

Stay open to critique.

When you have "blind spots" — or are usually unaware of your offenses — it's essential to hear others out while expressing their frustrations or calling you out.

This skill requires you to look past your current emotions and explore the scenario objectively while assuming other people's perspectives.

Enlist a therapist

It's always good to see a therapist when all is not working. People who go to therapy develop better skill sets for introspection and understand their weaknesses and fears more. Treatment also gives you a self-analysis level that, as an average person, you cannot reach on your own.

Once your ego is in check, move on to the next section.

Chapter 7: Proven Strategies for Overcoming Feelings of Guilt Alone

You may have nobody to turn to or don't want to share your problems with others for reasons best known to you. But you know that the guilt you feel keeps you stuck in life. Guilt echoes our regrets in life, takes away our peace of mind, and immobilizes us for a while, and overcoming it isn't always easy.

Some of us are so ashamed that we can't bring ourselves to tell anyone our secrets. So, the most overwhelming guilt plagues our souls with no chance for relief. To find out how to deal with it, continue reading.

But first, you should know that;

Sometimes, We Must Overcome Guilt by Ourselves

As I mentioned, to be in a position to forgive others, you need to forgive yourself. I know you feel bad for hurting others and regret it. But there is a way to forgive yourself. Forgiving yourself helps you look at your guilt differently and get closer to inner peace. I will teach you how to use some visualization techniques to help convince your subconscious mind to let go of the blame.

But first, allow me to say this;

Every time you delay taking the self-forgiveness pill, you block your progress. It is, therefore, essential to managing your remorse correctly to stop it from poisoning your entire mind, and it is vital to overcome guilt for optimum personal development.

So to help you overcome the guilt for wrongdoing, do as follows;

Name your guilt

Ignoring or pushing it away may seem like a smart move for now. But, like any other emotion, unaddressed guilt could intensify and worsen.

Snubbing your guilt may, in the meantime, keep it from spilling over your daily life, but hiding your emotions is only a temporary strategy. To truly address your guilt, you must first accept the feeling, however unpleasant.

Do this exercise:

With a journal to record your thoughts, sit alone somewhere quiet.

Tell yourself, or note what occurred:

"I feel terrible because I raised my voice at my kids."

"I lied to my boss."

"I didn't keep my word."

Let the guilt, regret, anger, frustration, and other emotions that might come up flow —writing down what you feel can help.

Sit with your feelings and walk through them with curiosity, not judgment. Many situations seem more complicated at first, but keep doing it.

Regular mindfulness (as shown later) and journaling can make a big difference if you have difficulty acknowledging guilt. Such practices can help you familiarize yourself with your emotions, making it easy to accept and navigate them, even the most painful ones.

Explore the source of your guilt

Before successfully navigating shame, you need to recognize where it comes from.

Of course, feeling guilty when you do something wrong is okay, especially when you know you are at fault.

It's likewise vital to remember not to blame yourself needlessly for things beyond your control. You may even feel guilty about having a fantastic job, and your best friend is unemployed or leaving a partner who is still concerned about you.

Guilt from unmet expectations doesn't even consider any effort you've dedicated to overcoming the present challenges derailing your success.

To recap, some familiar sources of guilt include:

- Surviving disaster or trauma

- Having conflict between your values and your choices

- Physical or mental health concerns

- Having desires or thoughts you consider wrong

- Focusing on meeting your own needs while you believe in putting others first

That said, you must first do some introspection and learn where your guilt originates. Use the previous ideas on sources of guilt and shame to help you with this.

Instead of self-blame, commit to self-kindness from now onwards.

Learn from the past

Some mistakes could cost you a loved one or close friend and feeling guilty or sad for losing someone or something is often inevitable. But no matter how bad you think you are, you cannot change the past. As discussed later, meditating or reminiscing your history won't fix what transpired.

Rewriting events by replaying them with different results won't help. However, it helps to consider further the lessons learned.

Ask yourself:

What caused the mistake? Explore any triggers that provoked your action and feelings that took you down the negative spiral.

What can you do differently now?

What do your actions tell you about yourself? Do they point to any specific behaviors you can work on?

Here are some general strategies for overcoming guilt.

Replace negative self-talk with compassion or yourself

If your internal dialogue is hostile, it can undermine and sabotage you. These internal messages come from your inner critic and significantly affect your feelings and behavior.

But what is this inner critic?

The voice you hear speaking to you from within is the inner critic. It is what judges, criticizes, or humiliates you. It tells you that; you are not good enough, you are fat, nobody likes you, you are not worthy of this, nobody cares about you, you don't have any friends or suggest mean things.

We all have an inner critic, but some of us have inner critics that are harsher than others. If you have a harsh inner critic, you probably grew up in an environment where people directly or indirectly said negative things about you. For instance, abandoned or abused people develop a cruel inner critic, as they usually deduce their experience as "there must be something wrong with me."

A hostile inner critic erodes our self-worth and confidence. Additionally, the flood of negativity from your inner critic can cause much distress. When it torments you for a long time, you can develop mental health problems like depression, anxiety, etc.

However, the inner critic can be a helpful tool. We can use its message to survive, spot potential external threats, and avoid embarrassment or failure. Furthermore, it can encourage you to push on and achieve your goals. It can also tell you what you can do to make things better.

Fortunately, irrespective of how harsh your inner critic is, there are ways to manage it and stop it from controlling your actions.

Show yourself some compassion. Guilt can trigger harsh self-criticism, which doesn't improve things. You may have to face the consequences for the wrong, but engaging in self-punishment can take a heavy emotional toll on you.

Rather than shaming yourself, consider what you would tell a friend in the same situation. You'd perhaps point out the good they've done and show them their strengths while letting them know you value them. Instead of self-blame, commit to self-kindness from now onwards.

Remind yourself that making mistakes doesn't mean you're nasty —We all mess up sometimes. When you find yourself in some circumstances, you may be to blame; always remember humans are to err, and we learn from our mistakes. You deserve kindness.

When you remind yourself that you are worthy, you increase your confidence, making it easy to be objective and not swayed by your emotional distress.

Observe and listen to what your inner critic is saying, and then let it go. Treat any useless messages like clatter and try to shift your attention from them.

Be aware of when your inner critic appears by proactively identifying places, events, times, and people that usually trigger your inner critic – stay prepared for it.

Acknowledge it will never go away. Accept that you will always have an ongoing internal dialogue with yourself that controls your thoughts and actions, and there is nothing wrong with that.

You must choose how to engage or react to your inner critic's negative aspect. Change your relationship with it so it becomes your friend rather than your foe.

Consider where the self-critical attitudes came from. Tracking down where your negative thoughts came from helps you gain more insight into them. Do past events or anything else trigger your negative thoughts or self-talk?

Step back from your criticism so you can observe it, weaken it and dis-identify yourself.

Use Humor as a way to Cope. When your inner critic shows up, imagine it's a cartoon or fictional character in a TV show or movie you find ridiculous, amateurish, or silly. Visualize that character you choose as your inner critic. It will be easy to ignore such a character.

Create an Action Plan to Overcome Guilt

Here is a format you can use to create a good action plan;

Define your problem

First, evaluate your situation. Do you feel guilty about one mistake, or are there more? Have you considered all possibilities? Explore all sources of guilt at this stage, and ask the others who are concerned or interested in helping you for their input in finding the problem.

Once you identify the problem, collect and examine data to validate or invalidate any assumptions you have made about yourself. Ask questions:

- *Why are you feeling guilty?*
- *Who can help you understand the situation better?*

☐   What part of my behavior do others (therapists, friends, bosses) say is offensive?

☐   How do others make me feel guilty? How can I handle them?

Compare your analyses and that of others.

Clarify and prioritize your problem(s); if there is more than one issue behind your guilt, you must prioritize and start with the most critical problem first. Ask questions to sort out your issues.

Where am I wrong?

Which mistake has the most damaging effects in terms of triggering guilt and hurting others?

What wrongdoing triggers a pang of lasting guilt?

Which mistakes have a short-term guilt effect on my mind?

In this case, we are stopping guilt, but we must first clarify what makes us guilty the most and prioritize finding its solutions.

Write a solution for each situation.

Find SMART solutions to stop the guilt.

S – Specific; give specific solutions to the actions that hurt others and trigger guilt. Say, I will do this and that.

M – Measurable; what indicators will show you that you have gotten rid of guilt? It could be when someone is ready to go out or date because it shows they have dealt with the remorse from a previously failed marriage.

A –Achievable; are your targets achievable or realistic within your abilities and responsibility? It may not be easy to achieve and require effort; perhaps you must get out of your comfort zone and push yourself.

R – Relevant; keep your solutions applicable to your current situation. For example, you may not be able to avoid the person who constantly criticizes you, but you can find ways to spend less time with them.

T – Timely; set a reasonable, flexible time frame for your changes, e.g. By next year, you will be free from guilt.

Implement your solutions

Apply the answers to the What? When? How? Where? Who?

List your resources; money to afford treatment fees, friends and relatives to support you, your willpower, etc.

Also, list your potential barrier to making progress; the harsh economy, a sick relative, unemployment, etc.

Use your action plan to stop the guilt.

Monitor and evaluate your progress

Your next step to solving your problem is to strategize on monitoring your results. Know if the solutions have solved your problem and note areas of improvement. Pick up another guilt-inducing problem, or redefine an old problem and always have an alternative explanation for each issue.

Remember, Guilt Can Work For You

Take guilt as an alarm that wakes you up to your mistakes and shows you that your choice contradicts your values. Instead of letting it overwhelm you, try putting it to work.

When you use it for self-improvement, guilt can reveal areas that make you feel dissatisfied.

Perhaps you are struggling with honesty and finally got caught in a lie. Maybe you would like to spend some time with your family, but something stops you.

Addressing such circumstances could get you back on track with your goals.

If you feel guilty for not enjoying some time with your friends, you could amp up your efforts to connect with others. You may improve the situation of a stressful relationship by devoting one day a week to your partner.

Paying attention to your guilt and establishing what it's conveying about you is worthwhile.

Regretting over hurting another could suggest you are empathetic and didn't mean to cause harm. If you are inclined to feel wrong about stuff beyond your control, finding the root cause of your guilt could be helpful.

Once you have your guilt figured out, move on to the next phase. Apply the strategies below to help you forgive yourself for what you have done that makes you guilty and ashamed.

For that matter, here are the following;

Three Strategies for Forgiving Ourselves For What We Have Done To Ourselves

When you can't move past the harm you have brought to yourself, consider the ideas below;

Define your remorse

Identify what is making you feel guilty and be honest with yourself. To forgive yourself, you've first to identify the particular hurts— decisions, mistakes, regrets behind your pain. Name the wrongdoing. It is best to list these wrongs down on paper. Specifically, label the specific hurtful words and actions you regret. Own everything you want to forgive yourself for, and allow some time to feel remorse.

Feel it!

Suppose you stole money, lied about it but got caught, your boss fired you, and you lost a career path you may never regain. That sucks. Allow yourself to be sad and heartbroken about your loss. Accept what is gone is gone and may never come back rather than dwelling on the "what ifs." Also, avoid making excuses for them—it is what it is. Cry if you want, but don't dwell on it.

Remember to reflect on the things you failed to do. For instance, thinking, "I should have gone back to college" or "I should have moved out when I had the chance" are signs of regret. Identify any pattern of behavior that has weighed you down for years. Reflect on significant life events plus subtle, day-to-day choices. Include the small stuff hurting you.

Once you have a comprehensive list, step back from it. How do you feel about acknowledging these mistakes?

Do you feel relieved or enlightened?

Are you scared?

Are you prepared to work on it?

Detach from your guilt for a moment

Another way to overcome guilt is to detach from it and view it from another angle. It will help you see mistakes differently and maybe develop a better approach to resolving them.

Here is an exercise to help you with this;

Imagine that you did not hurt yourself; somebody else did. So, this guilt is not yours; put it on that person's shoulders. Now take the judgment seat as you imagine the blame isn't yours. Write your ruling in detail about the punishment the person deserves, and also add reasons for mercy.

According to what you wrote, do they deserve punishment or forgiveness? Remember to show leniency as you would towards others in the same situation.

This exercise will give you a different perspective on your guilty feelings.

Reconcile with yourself

Reconciling means cleaning out your emotional closet—choosing acceptance and surrendering to a past you cannot change instead of criticizing yourself. It means that you choose to accept yourself with your uniqueness and flaws, not because you like whatever you did, but because you realize that self-loathing is not helpful anymore. You decide to stop treating yourself harshly and humiliating yourself with contempt; you do as you do to others in a similar situation.

Remember Mandela, Gandhi, and Mother Teresa as good examples of reconciliation with yourself because they taught that hatred of oneself is the worst of all transgressions.

That said, there are many ways you can reconcile with yourself, namely;

Gestures combined with gentle words

You can reconcile with yourself through gestures. Hug yourself and tell yourself some kind things to show compassion to ward off negativity and make it easier for you to accept yourself as you calm your nerves.

For example, hug yourself with your arms crossed above your chest and hands on the shoulder blades. Then say silently or audibly, "I forgive myself." And if you don't like this phrase for some reason, an alternative is, "It's okay the way it is. I am okay the way I am."

Laugh out loud or smile

Find something funny about what you have put yourself through and how things didn't turn out so bad. Smiling and laughing are effective for reducing negativity and lifting your moods.

According to numerous research studies, when you smile or laugh, your brain releases neuropeptide molecules to help drive away stress. Additionally, it produces neurotransmitters such as serotonin, dopamine, and endorphins. Endorphins work like mild pain relievers, whereas serotonin acts as an antidepressant. Dopamine makes you feel good.

Laugh because you have cried enough.

Write a letter to yourself.

You can also write a letter to yourself.

Writing a letter can be therapeutic for you. Since no one criticizes us the way we do ourselves, to silence your inner critic, talk to yourself like you would speak to a random person.

Do this exercise to help you with this.

Sit with a pen and paper. Now imagine a good friend telling you they can't forgive themselves for something terrible they've done —and it is the exact thing you're feeling guilty about doing. Now write a letter to your hurting friend, encourage them, build them up, and permit them to forgive themselves.

Here are some questions to help you formulate your letter well:

- Why is it okay to relieve yourself from your past? What are some of the benefits of doing so?

- What is helpful about this situation? For example, can I learn something from it?

- Are there gestures or words that would help them to forgive themselves easily?

Three Strategies For Forgiving Ourselves For What We Have Done To Others

Here are some ideas to help you forgive yourself for the harm you caused others through wrong behavior.

Admit to yourself

First, acknowledge by telling yourself that you own this; you are responsible for it and did it.

List the wrongs you feel guilty about one by one and get everything and everyone covered. Think about what you did—using the method we discussed earlier to identify your mistakes.

What decisions, errors, and regrets are behind your guilt? Reflect on what is so bad about your behavior or mistake—write it down on paper. Name what is hurting you about your behavior, and be very specific and honest. Remember to indicate whom you wronged.

Remember what you failed to do for that person before or after the mistake. For instance, thinking, "I should have said sorry," "I should not have let my son go alone on that day he had an accident," or "I could have held my tongue" are all signs of regret.

Identify any guilt that you could have entertained for years. Reflect on all the offenses you have committed and including minor stuff. Please don't ignore the small things. They are the most hurtful.

Once you have your brokenness well laid out, move on to the next step.

Switch places with the hurt person

To grasp the seriousness of what you did or said, attempt to view your offense from the eyes of the hurt person. Shifting your perspective can help you appreciate how the aggrieved person feels.

When we try to put ourselves in others' shoes, we acquire an understanding that allows us to be more supportive and patient with ourselves and others. Exercising empathy for yourself and others helps you to forgive yourself for the harm done quickly. When you only examine a situation from your perspective or experience, you may misjudge your motives or misinterpret your feelings, reactions, and actions.

Do this exercise;

Please take a minute to think about what you did to that person and how they are feeling, and imagine somebody doing something similar to you. Now take the judgment seat as you reflect on the wrong. Write down your ruling in detail about the punishment the person deserves and if you need to be merciful to them. According to what you wrote, does that person's behavior deserve the chastisement you have given yourself or forgiveness?

Would you like to offer some leniency?

Once you do this, you will know if torturing yourself is worth it, and consider treating yourself with compassion as you would another person who committed a similar offense.

Absolve yourself from the guilt

I am sure you don't want to live with the agony forever. The good news is that you can heal from this guilt and finally free yourself. Start with showing yourself more compassion and love. And, of course, proceed to make things right within yourself.

First, forgive yourself.

Stand or sit alone in a quiet place. It might look tacky, but when you're ready for it, I would like you to speak the following words loudly:

"I forgive myself for _____."

Own up to everything you did wrong to that person in your apology. Touch your heart and say thank you for doing that! Now hug yourself and remind yourself that you are a good person and love yourself.

Second, imagine that you are apologizing to the person. What would you tell them?

Write down an apology letter with everything you need to say. Include the things you overlooked before. Be very specific and sincere with your apology. Empty your heart on that paper. Now burn that paper as you imagine all the negative energy going away in smoke. Relieve yourself for the pain and hurt with a deep, long breath.

After your sincere self-repentance or unaided self-forgiveness, you can do some symbolic act for the offended.

To add to this;

The sure way to avoid guilt is to learn from your mistakes constantly. Take guilt as a wake-up call to heed life lessons to evolve and advance. And overcome it with a sincere heart and a mind eager for solutions instead of ignoring or muting guilt before hearing its entire message. After that, live a free being.

Now that you know how to overcome your guilt alone, move on to the next chapter to see how you can do it with others.

Chapter 8: Proven Strategies for Overcoming Feelings of Guilt with Others

Although you have made peace with yourself, you may feel that you need to approach the ones you hurt to try and make peace with them. As I said, feeling guilty for doing something terrible is usual and reasonable. However, because it can be a problem when the guilt lingers on, use the following techniques to get you started;

Acknowledge and Apologize

Accept the hurt you caused. Apologize and make amends. Say sorry immediately and unconditionally. Avoid trying to justify your behavior or shift blame, even though others are involved.

A sincere apology could help repair the damage of wrongdoing. By saying sorry, you express regret or remorse to the people you hurt and make them aware that you are working on avoiding making a similar mistake in the future.

You may not receive forgiveness instantly, as apologies do not mend ruined trust.

A genuine apology supports your healing, allowing you to air your feelings and accept your responsibility for messing up.

To give a successful apology, you may need to:

- Acknowledge your role
- Show remorse
- Avoid making excuses
- Ask for forgiveness

Finish off by showing that you regret your actions.

Make Amends Quickly

Try to make things right as soon as possible, and repent for your wrongdoing. Delaying to do so will only make guilty feelings accumulate and become unhealthy, triggering anxiety and other problems. Making amends implies that you have committed to change.

It is good to try and make amends for your actions by accepting that your actions hurt the person. For example, if you overlooked something significant, which your fellow employee had to work overtime to correct, you can explain yourself to the manager and take the blame.

Perhaps you're feeling guilty for not having some quality time with someone you love or not checking on them when they need support. To make the employee feel better, offer to help them with their tasks sometimes. After you apologize, ask the person, "How can I be there for you to demonstrate your will to change?"

Remember that if it's impossible to offer a direct apology because you cannot contact the person you hurt, write a letter instead. Pouring your apology on paper can be beneficial, even though they do not see it.

Change Your Behavior

If you continuously behave the same way, you must address your behavioral tendencies. A genuine apology may mean nothing when you fail to behave differently henceforth. Your behavior change should encompass ways of avoiding making the same mistake again.

Since feeling guilty can come from bad habits, which can be hard to break, I have a few ideas for breaking bad habits, and I'd suggest you start with awareness and being more mindful.

To begin the journey of breaking a bad habit, note:

- ☐ When does your terrible habit usually occur?
- ☐ Where are you?
- ☐ How often do you do it each day?
- ☐ What triggers the action and causes it to start?
- ☐ Who are you with?

Just tracking these few things can make you more aware of the behavior and give you more ideas for stopping it.

Consider the following questions to establish your behavioral patterns:

When was the last time (in months or years) you did something different?

Have I acted the same way in my past or present life under other circumstances?

If so, under what circumstances, exactly, do we have something in common?

Here's an easy way to get started: Track how many bad habits occur daily. Put a piece of paper and a pen in your pocket. Write down on a piece of paper each time a bad habit starts. Add up all your scores and check your total.

The first goal is not to judge yourself or feel guilty for doing something unhealthy and unproductive. The only goal is to recognize when and how often it happens. You can take hold of the situation by being aware of the problem.

Breaking bad habits takes time and effort, but most of all, it takes persistence. Most people who embark on breaking bad habits fail before it works. It may not succeed immediately, but it doesn't mean it won't succeed.

Here are a few ideas;

Realize when you behave badly

Your mind can control your actions, but your behavior is more observable than your mind. If you are interested in changing your thoughts and behavior patterns, it was probably the behavior that made you realize something was wrong.

Your main goal here is not to judge yourself or feel guilty for behaving in a harmful, destructive way. You only need to recognize when and how often it happens. When you are more aware of the onset of a bad habit, you are less worried about it reoccurring.

Here's an easy exercise to start: Track how many bad habits occur daily. Put a piece of paper and a pen in your pocket. Write down on paper each time a bad habit happens and when it happens. Later on in the evening, add up all your scores and analyze your result.

As taught later in this book, observe your behavior as you would do intrusive thoughts in a mindfulness exercise. Notice them with a non-judgemental attitude and see if you can spot any trends. Observe how you usually act and note how it makes others feel afterward, and remember to write down your observation and insight.

First, it helps you understand the sequence of events that lead to unwanted behavior and the isolated events that can cause a specific behavior. For example, you may exhibit unwanted behavior only when you're with a particular person, drinking, or having a bad day at work. By recognizing what mostly leads to undesirable behavior, you could break the chain of events that causes you to hurt others.

Second, it could help to refresh your memory on how your bad habits make you and others feel and maybe deeply convince you that your manners are unhelpful. Sometimes we contemplate engaging in harmful behaviors because we somehow forget how they make others feel.

Replace your bad habit with new ones.

Every behavioral pattern you have now has a reason in your life, good or bad. Sometimes, bad habits address specific needs in your life. In a way, these actions may benefit you even if they are wrong to other people.

For example, turning on your computer and immediately opening your email inbox might make you feel connected. At the same time, looking at all your emails can make you less productive, less attentive, and more stressful. But it protects you from FOMO (Fear of Missing Out), so you have to do it again.

Because of this, you would replace your bad habits with healthier ones that address that same need. For example, in the situation above, you can decide to create time for checking your mail and updating yourself on what is happening to avoid feeling guilty about it. You can also make it a habit to connect with loved ones offline to satisfy your need to feel connected.

Cutting out bad habits without replacing them leaves you with unmet needs, and it will be hard to "just don't do it" in the long run.

Accept and move on

After you've done everything you possibly can to make reparation and committed to not doing that again, you can proceed free of shame and guilt. You get more focused and productive as soon as you release guilt.

Overcoming Guilt in the Company of Others

Life is a series of events that do not always go your way. Remember that you are not alone when going through a difficult moment in your life. Looking around, you will notice that many people are willing to assist you. Even if you don't feel comfortable sharing your problems with your family and friends, you can visit anonymous platforms.

The first and most important reason you need to share your problems and stories of struggle with others is that you can act as a beacon of hope for each other. Struggling is a part of life, but it doesn't mean you must suffer alone. If you share your problems with other people going through a similar thing, you can exchange ideas regarding how to go through it or handle it the right way.

Admitting your errors and troubles requires bravery since you expose your vulnerability to others. However, if you open up to others and show them who you are, you can form a strong relationship with them.

If you are genuine to yourself and others, you will receive a lot of support, giving you a great lift. Everyone wants to be loved and supported. Finding out that there are people who believe in you has a significant impact. It inspires you to take the next step in your endeavors.

If you share your concerns and sufferings with others, they will develop a soft spot for you and realize how difficult your life is. When the time comes, they will root for you and encourage you to achieve your goals.

Why share your guilt?

First, your mental dialogue can become customary to you as you get so used to your critical inner voice tearing you down and blaming you for practically everything that you hardly notice it's happening. Sometimes you may not even see that you are blaming yourself for things. You can't even realize that you are harsh on yourself.

Remember that you need to know you are blaming yourself before forgiving yourself. When you talk to your friend or close relative about your thoughts, they can help in identifying any unhelpful thinking patterns. They can quickly help you notice when you are blaming yourself for stuff that isn't especially your fault.

Second, overcoming guilt with others gives you a chance to come clean and let the person you hurt know that you feel terrible about what you did. They may think you are such a coldhearted person for doing what you did, especially if you walked away or kept quiet after that.

But in reality, they have no idea how much you have suffered because of what you did to them. Facing them allows you to make them understand what circumstances could have triggered your harmful acts towards them—in case they ask why you did that to them. It is finally your opportunity to speak to the issue and clear some misconceptions about the whole situation.

Let us now look at some strategies for overcoming guilt that leverage other's input;

Three Strategies That Allow Others to Forgive Us for What We Have Done to Ourselves

Appreciate the complexity of human behavior

As we saw earlier, we develop programmed reactions during childhood and as young adults. From an earlier age, we form extremely subtle learned behavioral patterns and may often handle situations relative to our earlier programming.

Knowing that we come from different backgrounds with diverse upbringings that can make our behavior complex, we understand that most things we say or do could have come from our earlier experiences or things beyond our control. Our automated responses continue to affect us and those around us.

They influence how we make decisions, manage frustration, and deal with challenges as adults. So make the people you hurt understand and appreciate that human behavior is complex, and it is not easy to understand why we do what we do.

By letting others know that there are things that somehow obscure human behavior, we open their eyes to seeing us as just human.

Evoke empathy and compassion

Since others don't know what you have been through, they can act indifferent toward you. But, when people understand why you do what you do to yourself and others, they can develop empathy instead of turning a cold shoulder toward you.

For instance, upon seeing sex workers, we may wonder why they take the risk of engaging in prostitution, exposing themselves to getting STIs, and being abused. If they explained that they are poor and desperate, with no other form of employment despite their efforts to secure one, and would change their behavior if given better opportunities. That story may compel us to try to put ourselves in their shoes and understand that we probably would have done the same in a similar or worse situation.

Therefore when you clarify your situation, you can evoke empathy and compassion in others. You help them understand your suffering and feel your pain so they could even want to help you somehow. With their support, you can let go of all the physical and emotional torture you have carried through the years.

Express your past trauma

Your added self-knowledge makes it easy to explain any past traumatic experiences that could make you behave in a certain way. You can explain to others who may be wondering about your hurtful actions and tell them about your past traumas that could be influencing your current behavior.

For instance, suppose you grew up in a family where criticism and scolding were normal responses. Your caregivers harshly criticized you for making mistakes and did not allow you to express negative emotions. If you are not careful, you could repeat such behavior with others and yourself leaving you feeling horrible.

For others to know why you criticize and hurt yourself, it is best to express your traumatic past to them. This added information could help them understand you better (why you behave the way you do) instead of judging or condemning you further.

Three Strategies That Allow Others to Forgive Us for What We Have Done to Them

Remind them that human is to err

Try to change others' perspectives about you by showing them that although you were wrong, nobody is immune to error (even them). Then, proceed to let them know that we are all not perfect and are bound to make mistakes and hurt people.

You can also politely point out that they make mistakes like you. Ask them to think about when they make mistakes and how they feel. Wouldn't they also like to be forgiven?

Doing this can make them change their attitude, accept your shortcomings or mistakes as part of human life, and even consider forgiving you.

Express how your good intentions went bad

Good intentions go wrong now and then. For example:
- Congratulating someone for pregnancy when they are not pregnant
- Predicting someone's age as much older than the person is while trying to give a compliment.
- Gift x-large clothing to a medium-sized person who gets offended (maybe you thought the person likes a little room).
- Surprising someone with a birthday party who happens to hate surprises.
- Telling someone their fly was open while it wasn't (I guess it was an optical illusion).
- Give a scented soap to someone who takes it like their body scent is foul (it seems you can't win).

The list of good intentions gone bad goes on and on, and we will always do or say offensive things unintentionally.

What is essential is explaining yourself to those hurt by your behavior.

Expressing your good intentions to stop hurting others' feelings is essential. It is where you let the person know that you did not intend to hurt them and did so by mistake.

In our previous example, when I hit my partner with my elbow by mistake, I quickly said sorry and tried to explain that I was getting into bed in a rush and did not think I would hit them. This way, although I hurt their head, I avoided a fight and hurt feelings.

So please do your best to explain your honest intentions that hurt them. Once you convince them that what you did or said was neither planned nor deliberate, they can bring themselves around to forgive you.

Mention that you didn't know better

Express your most profound regret about what happened. In your explanations, mention that you did your best based on your experience and knowledge. Had you known better, you wouldn't have behaved so anyway.

Getting the matter out into the open this way can considerably remedy the situation. Remember that you must admit your regrets and be responsible for your actions.

Expressing your regret is saying something like;

"I wish I didn't comment badly about your hairstyle."

"I feel awful for failing to show up /offending you /letting you down."

"I can't believe that I broke your best coffee mug."

Explain where it went wrong. For instance, "I didn't know you had cancer, and that hair issues were too sensitive for you; I don't know why I thought you'd find it hilarious."

"I knew I was already late, so I wrongly assumed you had left and decided not to show up altogether."

Or, "I was cleaning the cup for you, but it fell by mistake on the floor and broke."

Then, acknowledge your responsibility for it. Say something like, "I made a mistake." "I was very wrong about ____." "I know I owe you a huge apology." "I ought to have taken more care when washing the ceramic cup."

Show some signal that you will not repeat the same mistake. You could say, "Now that I know that hurts you, I will think more before speaking or doing that next time and be more considerate about your feelings."

We talked about the inevitability of mistakes and that as long as we live, we will find ourselves in the wrong in one way or the other. We also mentioned that when we make a mistake, we might continue feeling guilty throughout life, even if we apologize, repair the damage caused, and others forgive us for the harm we caused. We also discussed ways to cope with self-loathing and other negative emotions and finally let them go.

However, after you have forgiven yourself and cleared the guilt and shame, you need to be vigilant so that the feelings don't return. In the next chapter, we'll discuss how to do this.

Chapter 9: How to Prevent Self-Loathing from Returning

For some of us, even after going through the entire self-forgiveness process, feelings of guilt can return if we are not careful.

In short;

The guilt may go away but can return in subtler and more dangerous forms.

Guilt can find its way back into your head, camouflaged in other ways, like guilt-tripping, gaslighting, depression, and anxiety.

For that matter, let's discuss how to avoid feeling guilty.

How to Avoid Guilt and Keep It Away

Some things we often do make us prone to guilt. You should therefore avoid such traps as much as possible. To prevent you from harboring more guilt than before, here are some strategies:

Avoid setting unrealistic standards or expectations

Setting standards and expectations that are too high could make you feel guilty about not living up to them. Also, avoid living according to others' standards or expectations. If you continue to uphold other people's opinions, you may start feeling remorse for losing your control and probably disappointing them.

So, it's okay if you haven't mastered baking bread during the Covid-19 lockdown or you failed to respond to each message in your inbox today. Maybe you forgot to place an order for your week's groceries; either way, there is a tomorrow! Block out feelings of guilt every minute you fail to meet your expectations.

Only make those promises you can keep

Sometimes, we may make promises we know we can't keep, not because we don't respect or value others but because we have difficulty saying "no." Other reasons for breaking promises include carelessness, commitment issues, conflicting beliefs, and unreachable expectations.

Feeling guilty is typical after failing to fulfill our pledges or commitments. So, to avoid the guilt that follows broken promises or commitments, don't over-promise or over-commit.

Don't entertain self-blame

Assuming everything you or others do is your fault or problem is no way to live. Disassociate from anybody who shames, blames, judges, and unfairly criticizes you.

Stop measuring yourself against others. Constantly comparing yourself to others, particularly fashion icons or celebrities, is the quickest way to develop a negative body image and spiral into self-loathing. You are only responsible for how you appear to yourself and nobody else.

Challenge obsessive beliefs and avoid being self-judgmental or critical when you fail at something. When your general performance frustrates you, remind yourself that a lot could be happening in your life. Pressuring yourself may trigger guilt for not living up to your mostly impractical values.

Stop using guilt as a motivation or punishment tool

Harboring guilt is not easy; the more you utilize it for behavioral reinforcement, the more it returns. Avoid making others feel guilty as a punishment for wrongdoing or not doing what you want. As you try to dictate or control others' lives, the guilt usually boomerangs, and you can start feeling remorseful for your actions.

Prioritize tasks

At the core of guilt is conflicting priorities. Not having adequate time or ability to accomplish all the crucial tasks could result in regret. That is why you need to plan your activities in detail. Please start with your most critical duties and assign them a due date (or time) to help you prioritize.

Prioritizing tasks demands good decision-making skills. First, take some time to contemplate your decision and avoid making hasty decisions because you may feel guilty for your irrational choices later. Second, when you make a decision, stand firm by it. Avoid second-guessing your choice once you've decided to follow a particular path. Respect the one who made that choice (yourself).

For example, at work, you can start by listing your present duties and plot them on a grid x-axis representing importance and the y-axis urgency. Also, estimate (using apps) the time you use on each task. Go through your chart, and if you discover some chores are neither necessary nor urgent but very strenuous, scrap them off your to-do list.

Note the most critical jobs, start working on them and consider delegating some duties or requesting help if you don't have time or knowledge. We often hesitate to ask for help because we fear rejection or think it could undermine or diminish our status. Research shows that when we request others' service, they may like us more (it looks like a win-win situation for us!). You can handle other commitments and priorities with fewer things to do and reduce those annoying, guilt-inducing voices that accompany failure or procrastination.

Avoid being self-judgmental or critical when you fail to do some things. When your general performance frustrates you, remind yourself that a lot is happening in your life. Pressuring yourself may trigger guilt for not living up to your mostly impractical values.

Although it could take a while, you can learn these ways to decrease your overall feelings of guilt and instill them in your daily life. The earlier you start, the higher the chance for more balanced future generations.

The above techniques can come in handy for preventing guilt from sneaking back into your life. However, there are many other ways. It would help if you kept a hawk eye on your inclination to regret and then considered laying down an action plan to help you avoid any decisions or choices that could lead you back to the cycle of shame.

Build a long-term battle plan

If you are highly susceptible to experiencing guilt, creating a battle plan can help fight guilt every other day.

Here are three steps that you can use:

Create a guilt list

A guilt list is a list of everything that makes you feel guilty quickly. To help, ask yourself the following:

What do I tend to feel guilty about mostly?

What can I do to minimize my bad feelings about such stuff?

Being specific about what makes you always feel guilty may help you lay the groundwork down for preventing or overcoming guilt.

Lastly, next to every item you listed, write what you could do today to help eliminate or lessen your guilt.

Recognize your core values

Write your core values in another list. These are beliefs that are most significant to you in life.

Ask yourself:

- ☐ What is essential to me?
- ☐ What do I highly value in life?
- ☐ How do I start living in line with my values today?

Your values are your priorities. They are your main foundations for building your actions and decisions.

When something conflicts with your values, you may experience guilt. It generally implies that you have defied your core values. So, your values must be clear, especially if you are often guilty about stuff. Therefore, to stop guilt from returning to your life, begin by intentionally deciding to live consistent with your core values daily.

Create an action plan for lessening the guilt

Use the ideas in the previous chapter to create a structure or plan that consolidates these elements helping to minimize guilt and allowing you to achieve your expectations and set standards.

This action plan should help you maintain your core values consistently. The action plan needs to be "priority-driven" besides aligning with the top priorities in life (based on your core values).

Such an action plan will help improve your decision-making and hopefully gradually allow you to minimize your guilt tendencies successfully.

The Need To Remove Those Things Which Remind You of Guilt

Some of us say we want to let go, yet we keep needless baggage from our past. We hold on to memories of our former selves rather than starting life on a clean slate. The minute you commit to self-forgiveness, it is best to leave all your extra baggage behind because clinging to memories could revive guilty feelings and hinder self-forgiveness.

Discard stuff that reminds you of terrible things you did. Keeping things that make you feel guilty and constantly remind you of the bad things you did makes it challenging to move forward.

Once you have forgiven yourself, you need to discard, burn, eliminate or destroy some things; it's NOT an option.

Start by identifying anything that reminds you of a past you want to forget or triggers feelings of guilt or shame, such as; conversations or topics, places, smells, people or personalities, activities, clothes, dates, photos or images, stressful stuff, etc.

Then clean out ALL those things connecting you to your former unhappy self, things reminding you of the days before you changed. Eliminate those reminders of what existed BEFORE you chose self-forgiveness and decided to show yourself compassion and love.

For instance, get rid of everything (photos, clothes, places, etc.) that remind you of the days you want to forget because they were self-destructive and make you feel guilty and ashamed when you flashback.

Moreover, eliminate anything that exacerbates your grief of a loved one whose death you blame yourself for.

Try to dissociate the things you can't get rid of from their bad memories. Researchers suggest that specific proteins stimulate brain cells to make new connections to stored memories. The more you think about a particular event, the stronger the neural connections and the more intense the memory. So if you experienced a traumatic event when you were young, your fear might increase every time you remember it. Let's briefly see the chemistry behind this.

How does our memory work?

Our brain encodes (absorbs) information, stores it, and retrieves (recalls) it when needed. It either stores the info on short-term or long-term memory.

Information in our short-term memories quickly evaporates from our brains, but some seeps into our long-term memory, which has limitless storage space. Recreating certain sounds, smells, and sights around us can bring a long-term memory to the surface, even one we'd rather forget.

While our brains can easily forget ordinary stuff, it often stores any information attached to our strong emotions. [Several studies](#) established that people mostly recall information tied to positive or negative emotions more than emotionally neutral information.

Unfortunately, bad memories tend to stand out more than good ones, and the stronger the feeling attached, the more details you can remember. Researchers conclude that because bad memories interact powerfully with our often negative emotions, they are not easy to eliminate.

As Shaheen Lakhan, a certified neurologist, put it, forgetting something has a lot to do with managing the emotions attached to the memory. That's why many techniques for tackling bad memories emphasize gradually disassociating our memories from negative emotions.

You may want to forget a memory for various reasons. Some memories may embarrass you, while others might be more traumatic or distressing. Perhaps you don't want to recall specific people or past events as you carry out your day's responsibilities.

Maybe you are replaying a talk with your boss and beating yourself up whenever you imagine your discussion or what you said, and you don't like it because rerunning the scene adds to your worry about saying something wrong.

Or perhaps you can't stop pondering the names people called you when you were a child, and their hurtful comments still haunt you whenever you are in silence or meet new people.

For some people, memories wane with time. But, when you have an anxiety-related disorder like social anxiety disorder or a trauma-related condition such as post-traumatic stress disorder (PTSD), you may relive past moments you prefer to forget. The sudden recurrence of particular memories can be disturbing and debilitating and cause us to feel worse.

Regretful memories can creep into your consciousness even when you don't want them and make you feel more shame and guilt. Many researchers continue dedicating their resources in search of methods to help us intentionally forget. While they may not altogether remove unwanted memories from your mind, such methods can help stop bad memories from disturbing your life.

That brings us to...

How to Forget Things on Purpose

Considering that guilt and shame are triggered mainly by bad memories, let us discuss a few measures you can take to forget a memory—or at least decrease its impact.

Identify your memory. This idea may sound contradictory, but you must first remember something to forget it. What sounds, sights, and feelings are attached to that memory?

Process your emotions. Instead of avoiding all unwanted feelings accompanying the memory, allow yourself to feel them. A therapist may help you tackle emotions.

Pay attention to triggers reviving your memory. Notice what triggers your memory. Perhaps whenever you visit a place you used to go to with your ex-partner, the recollections of your painful breakup come to mind. Or, it could be the chicken soup smell that reminds you of your late mom and overwhelms you with her funeral tributes.

Try to substitute the memory. Your brain will eventually learn to replace any unpleasant memory with a different, better one. It is good to swap your attention with healthier alternatives than trying to suppress those memories.

For example, when you visit the place you went to with your ex-partner, try to think of the good times you had there instead of fixating on the breakup memory.

Adopt a healthier lifestyle. Inadequate sleep and excess stress could trigger unpleasant memories, so ensure you get enough sleep, exercise, and eat a wholesome diet. Maintaining a healthy lifestyle can boost your overall health.

Note: Forcing yourself to forget about something may backfire—and make you mull over it even more. A better way is to distract yourself by finding a task to keep you busy: call a friend and discuss a different subject, exercise, or do household tasks. Move around to enable you to "change the channel" and stop stewing over disturbing memories.

As you work on forgetting bad memories, it's good to explore them further. I will give you practical ideas for making unwanted memories seem more manageable and less daunting.

But first, let us explore;

Dangers of ruminating on bad memories

Regretful memories can creep into your consciousness even when you don't want them and make you feel more shame and guilt.

Some dangers include:

☐ Unhealthy coping skills: Studies show that rumination increases mental distress and your probability of engaging in harmful habits such as alcohol abuse or overeating.

☐ Worsen mental problems: Dwelling on your past mistakes, difficulties, or hardships could intensify depression, anxiety, OCD, and post-traumatic stress disorder.

☐ Perpetual negative thinking: Gradually, your negative beliefs become a habit that is tough to break. Even in the face of good stuff, being positive might be challenging.

The good news is that you can rewire your brain and dissociate it from past programming. So, if you've realized that your mind is constantly bringing up remorseful memories, don't worry.

All you need to do is to train your brain to create new neural pathways for better coping skills. It takes dedication and practice to reprogram your mind; you will have better days than others. But, provided you continue working on it, you shall make progress.

How to Tackle Unwanted Memories

If you usually beat yourself up when you remember your past mistakes or traumas, you need to change how you think. It may take a while to end rumination, but once you start managing it, you feel and behave better. Do the following;

Know when it's happening

Is your unwanted memory likely to arise in specific circumstances? Or do certain people, surroundings, or things, revive a particular memory? Be conscious of your thoughts and identify trends.

Understanding your memory better helps you know how to address it. Identify what provokes you to rehash and replay painful memories. Rather than avoid those triggers, learn practical coping methods. Find an alternative idea that is positive and more productive.

Reflect on solutions to your problems to avoid getting stuck in a negative thought cycle. Work on solving your problems and learning from your mistakes.

Expose yourself to possible triggers

Behavioral therapists suggest that exposure is an excellent coping mechanism for bad memories. Studies also show that exposure therapy can help treat phobias, Social Anxiety, OCD, and PTSD. To overcome negative emotions associated with something or someone, try exposure therapy, which involves gradually exposing yourself to whatever you fear. Directly face a situation, object, or activity you fear.

Suppose a dog bit you as a kid. You could now have a fear of dogs. You can try to touch a dog (in the presence of its master or a therapist) to overcome your fear of dogs. Memories triggering your fear can gradually become more tolerable with time as you expose yourself to dogs in a secure, organized way.

Suppose you fell on the stage while performing to a large audience and feel embarrassed to go back on stage. You could try to present to a smaller familiar audience and grow from there.

If you have a traumatic past, you could try to remember and describe your traumatic experience (perhaps during meditation) to reduce the negative feelings associated with it.

Set aside some time for yourself

In our busy world, the mind is constantly being dragged from pillar to pillar, cluttered with emotions and thoughts, leaving us overworked, stressed, and somewhat anxious.

Most of us don't take five minutes to sit and unwind, let alone thirty minutes or more for meditation. However, our well-being needs a few minutes to cultivate our spiritual expansion and attain an improved mind-body balance.

To process stuff happening in your everyday life, have some "thinking time" in your schedule. When you contemplate or worry outside that scheduled time, remind yourself, "I'll think about that later." Set aside 20 minutes daily to think, reflect or worry about stuff.

Knowing you have a chance to ponder a distressing topic later can help you postpone it. Sticking to your time limit will help you think about your problems more flexibly while also preventing you from punishing yourself by rehashing your painful memories repeatedly.

In your reflective time alone, you can also;

Practice mindfulness

Mindfulness can eliminate negative thoughts connected to your guilt-inducing memories. Mindfulness is a practice for cultivating awareness to help block distractions and intrusive thoughts and keep your mind in the present moment (here and now). If you're a busy bee like me, you can use simple mindfulness exercises to clear your mind and get much-needed rest during a chaotic day.

Here is a Mindfulness exercise;

Sit with a pen and paper somewhere quiet, observe your thoughts, detect negative thoughts/beliefs and note them down. Don't judge.

Analyze and see how nasty some thoughts are. For each negative review, write a positive one to counter it. Repeat this whenever a negative feeling or thought arises.

You can practice mindfulness during meditation or in the middle of other activities such as queuing, showering, washing dishes, gardening, cleaning, etc. Bring mindful, unbiased attention to your present moment. Pay full attention to whatever you are doing and block distracting thoughts. Feel your body's sensation as you go on with your activities.

Note: All relaxation techniques, including deep breathing, meditation, progressive muscle relaxation, and guided imagery, can help lessen unwanted memories' harmful effects. Combined with gradually exposing yourself to your triggers, they can help you discover new ways of calming your reactions to bad memories.

Try self-acceptance

Perfectionism often makes memories look more distressing. If you always need to appear perfect, memories of past mistakes could make it challenging to forge ahead.

If your memories center around mistakes, try doing the wrong things on purpose. In time, memories of such situations will acquire a different flavor once you get used to embarrassing yourself.

Practicing self-acceptance may help dull the impact of bad memories. Affirm that you are now worthy of acceptance rather than waiting until you become a "perfect" person.

Once you apply the above strategies, you will soon be free to live more passionately without those memories. Remember, those bad memories don't define or control who you are and only reduce your power. They are part of your past.

Hanging onto them holds you back. So, switch off from them and ensure to remove all the toxicity in your life; as we mentioned, thoughts, people, and negative news that make you feel guilty for nothing should not be part of your life. Maintaining a guilt-free living will be effortless when not bogged down by baggage.

Once you eliminate the guilt-inducing stuff, you can move on to using mantras to help you maintain your new positive state.

The Need for Mantras to Manage Your Guilt

Many traditions have used mantras for thousands of years effectively as an alternative treatment for emotional challenges, depression, anxiety, and several mental health disorders. Repeating a few phrases to yourself, such as "This event does not define me," can remind you of your power. Before we explore such words further, let us cover some basics.

What do mantras entail?

Like most people, when you think of mantras, you may imagine people sitting in a yoga pose repeating the "om" sound with their eyes closed, and you are somewhat correct. However, "om" is not the only mantra.

So what are mantras?

A mantra is a sound, phrase, or word believed to trigger positive feelings or promote general well-being, usually applied during mindfulness meditation.

Even if they seem similar to positive affirmations, mantras are shorter, powerful statements or words intended to motivate and inspire positive action or behavior change. Still, a fine line exists between affirmations and mantras. So, rhythmically repeating affirmations or phrases to improve your concentration, meditation, or grounding is a fusion of these two tools.

If you need a little convincing, let us look at some scientifically approved benefits of using mantras.

Benefits of mantras

Although research to understand the part mantras play therapeutically is ongoing, some researchers have already confirmed their benefits. According to a 2018 scientific review, using mantras might benefit your emotional and mental well-being. They also provide an excellent supplementary treatment for mental disorders since they use words to evoke positive feelings without any side effects.

Additional research on the effects of sound and listening to music suggested that practicing mind-body techniques could increase biomarkers linked with better cognition, mood, and sleep.

Note: Mantras can help manage many mental health symptoms, but you should not forego orthodox mental health therapies. So, consider reaching out to a mental health professional for any issue concerning your mental health. They can diagnose your conditions and offer a suitable treatment plan.

All in all, mantras are helpful tools for stopping guilt, and I will share with you several simple mantras that have helped me conquer guilt.

Mantras for Depression

Include;

'My feelings are valid.'

As covered earlier, depression sometimes causes unnecessary shame. Recognizing your feelings as valid could help drive out such shame and empower you to control your depression.

Consider chanting 'My feelings are valid' out loud or intone it when depression triggers any destructive self-loathing feelings.

'I deserve to feel better.'

Use the above mantra to remind yourself that you matter. It does help encourage positive thinking about yourself and lessens the unworthiness that accompanies depression.

Although you can verbalize this mantra anytime, it's handy when unsure whether to visit a mental health expert to diagnose and cure depression.

Mantras for Anxiety

Include;

'Right now, I am OK.'

Anxiety can make you have irrational fears or worries about your life and find it hard to be in the present moment. It would help if you reminded yourself that you are okay.

Repeat this mantra when you have an intense anxiety spell to help ground and jolt you back to the present. But remember to chant it continuously until your anxious feelings go.

'My mind is creating this — it is not my reality.'

Use this mantra to remind yourself that what you think may not be accurate. Saying so can help lower your anxiety, making you feel empowered to cope better.

Repeat this mantra when you feel worried or fearful about the future or when negativity engulfs your mind.

Mantras for Mental Clarity

Include;

'Not my circus, not my monkeys.'

Sometimes the intrusive thoughts are about others' problems — not yours. Other people's problems can make us feel guilty for being unable to help solve them. So, it's essential to identify what you can help with and ignore anything you cannot help to improve your much-needed clarity.

Use this mantra when others divulge their problems expecting you to help and you are not in a position to or when you are straining to overlook others' issues and focus on your own. Ensure you intone it to avoid hurting others' feelings.

'One thing at a time.'

Sometimes you may have a lot on your to-do list and limited time. Often, we are too optimistic—we start the day full of expectations to get all kinds of things done. Our unrealistic expectations can cause anxiety, guilt, and shame if we fail to accomplish our tasks.

A good strategy for tackling your endless to-do list is reminding yourself to stop and handle one thing at a time.

Repeat this mantra to help you during stressful moments at work or when feeling overwhelmed by tasks and lacking time to do them.

Soothing Mantras

Include;

'I give myself permission to rest.'

Our crazy work schedules and everyday demands can cause burnout or mental problems. This mantra can help to reaffirm your mind that it's OK to take a breather and watch out for yourself.

Do this mantra right before you relax, while on vacation, or when you are guilty of taking your most deserved rest.

"I am willing to see this differently."

When saying this mantra, you abandon your narrow worldview. You acknowledge that you are stuck and that what you're feeling or seeing at the moment is not good. But you are willing to work on it, understand it differently, and change your perception and perspective.

You don't want to change circumstances. Instead, you are willing to see things in a new light and open to new insights.

'Om'

Research recommends using this common mantra in meditation makes you feel calm and less anxious. It's considered a primal sound that vibrates your entire body.

If you want to integrate this mantra into your daily routine, this video, "Right Ways to Chant OM" by Dr. Hansaji Yogendra, can teach you much more about this technique.

"I love you."

This mantra can reawaken compassion and self-love. It can evoke peace within you rather than sadness. Say this mantra as you wash dishes, walk, brush teeth, queue, or whatever else. Repeat it ceaselessly so you slowly start persuading yourself to love yourself.

Remember that guilt is that feeling of doing (or assuming) wrong and a desire to undo or minimize the damage caused by the wrong. However, since some people can instill guilt unnecessarily—let's see how that happens in the next chapter and how it deters self-forgiveness.

Chapter 10: People Who Inhibit Your Self-Forgiveness

Do you have people who always make it hard for you to move past your mistake by always re-introducing more guilt in you?

Well, we have all met people who try to make us feel guilty for no reason in one way or another, and while some do that unconsciously, others are more deliberate. When people constantly instill guilt in us, they make it hard for us to forgive ourselves.

Toxic people, for instance, often use *guilt tripping* as the primary guilt-inducing tactic.

But what is it exactly?

Guilt tripping is when someone tries to make you feel guilty for something indirectly. It is a passive-aggressive behavior arising from the person's inability or unwillingness to communicate honestly, openly, and assertively.

People can use this manipulation tactic to make you feel bad or compel you to do what they want by inducing guilt, like when someone shames you with comments that leave you feeling inadequate, accused, and condemned.

Allowing others to express themselves when we hurt or disappoint them with our behavior is good, but it becomes an issue when the conversation gets manipulative or passive-aggressive. Open communication (that is NOT guilt-tripping) is, for example, when someone says, "Hey, I know we can be late sometimes. However, when you show up late every time, I usually feel like you do not prioritize our time together."

Often guilt-tripping comes from people closest to you, including friends, family members, romantic partners, bosses, or coworkers. To know when someone is engaging in guilt-tripping, observe the following typical signs:

- Comments and behavior intended to make you feel bad or guilty

- Refusal to say what's wrong but acting upset

- Giving the impression that you owe them for something or you are a terrible person

- Airing negative views about you indirectly

- Spilling your entire "history" of past mistakes

Before we look at those who are more intentionally manipulative, let us explore subtle ways people guilt-trip us into doing what they want.

Usually, without ill intentions, our loved ones can guilt trip us and make us feel bad:

Example 1

When I was younger, I often visited my grandparents. We shared meals and talked about school, work, and life, which would make me feel nurtured and loved. But when I finally got ready to leave, my grandfather said sentimentally, "It was so nice having you here. Maybe you'll stay longer next time."

I now know that Grandpa was letting me know he appreciated my regular visits and perhaps tried to entice me to spend more time with them. I also know it would be devastating if he discovered that his words almost ruined my stay. Immediately he said that a burst of remorse engulfed me that afternoon or evening and filled me with guilt. I thought, "Should I extend my stay a little? Was I a self-centered, heartless grandchild?

Example 2

Suppose you have a dinner date planned with your partner. You have already made reservations at a fancy restaurant. But, at the eleventh hour, you receive an emergency call concerning a beloved family member that needs your immediate attention. You, therefore, must cancel the evening plans.

In this case, your partner's guilt-tripping reaction may sound like, "It's okay; I'll dine alone. After all, you're always too busy for me." This response can invoke guilt and leave you feeling awful for canceling the date, despite having a legitimate reason.

Often, regardless of your efforts to give the guilt-inciter what they're demanding, it's never enough. Your guilt-monger often goes up the ante and wants more, making you feel sad, inadequate, irritated, frustrated, and squashed.

Sadly, the people who try to trigger guilt in others suffer along with their targeted person. Sometimes, it's not easy to see that those trying to incite guilty feelings in us suffer too because often, they tend to be angry and manipulative and can put out their guilt-stirring words with a smile.

But their behavior often hides other vulnerable emotions. Underneath their guilt-inciting behavior often lurks loneliness, sadness, neediness, and hurt. Unfortunately, their behavior frequently produces the opposite of what they want. Instead of giving them the affection or love they desperately wish for, they push them away.

And that brings us to people who deliberately induce guilty feelings in others. Some of the most dangerous guilt-trippers are selfish people like narcissists and haters.

So, let's talk about...

The Narcissism Epidemic

Maybe you are surrounded by narcissists, and you don't know. But you must be aware of narcissists to learn how to deal with them. So then;

Who is a narcissist?

A narcissist is a person diagnosed with a personality disorder known as narcissism, symbolized by excessive pride, lowered guilt-conscience, zero empathy, and hunger for admiration. A narcissist is good at manipulation, shifting personalities to attract more attention, and trying to look good in front of others.

When you are the narcissist's target, you can suffer badly. They can abuse you in subtle ways that often seem to be in your best interest. Their abuse focuses on emotional manipulation, which may leave you with no physical marks but affect you more profoundly. Their main aim is to control how you think and act through;

Shifting the blame onto you

According to research, selfish people often assume a victimhood approach to life, which is why they can do something wrong and transfer fault or shift blame towards you, another person, or external factors. Their defensiveness and blame-shifting might sound like this:

"I wouldn't have done that if you didn't do this."

"You knew what you got into; that is just how I am."

"It's not my fault—I did it because of you /stress/money/work."

If you can't notice when someone plays the victim card, you might feel unnecessarily guilty and over-apologize for slight errors.

Ridiculing you

Narcissists might find it challenging to hold positive and negative feelings for someone simultaneously. They may verbally abuse you with insults, shaming, belittling criticisms, and sarcastic behaviors such as laughing as you talk and dog-whistling (making public comments they know are offensive, shameful, or critical to you, although seemingly neutral.)

Consequently, when you get into an argument with such people, they say things like;

- "That's stupid."
- "Something is wrong with you."
- "You're so crazy."

Gaslighting

Studies suggest that people with narcissism aren't prone to feeling guilty, which can make them refuse to be accountable for their behavior. Consequently, they may out rightly deny having said or done something hurtful, a tactic called gas lighting.

Gas lighting is a more profound manipulation tactic where a person refuses to own up to their mistake, despite proof. Their behavior can make you question yourself, second-guess your decisions, doubt your sense of reality, put you at fault, and make you feel guilty.

It could sound like this:

- "That never happened."
- "I never said that."
- "This doesn't prove anything."

Gas lighting may not be completely obvious. It can involve deflecting tactics to confuse you or complicate the issue.

Deflecting arguments

When you face a narcissist with concrete evidence (like receipts, e-mails, and photos), they may redirect your attention away from them and towards you as a distraction.

Deflection consists of the following:

- Indirect answers or no-answers: dragging irrelevant issues into discussions.

- Prior arguments: digging up old matters, mostly your previous "wrongdoings."

- Guilt-tripping: "Is this how you repay me after all I've done for you?"

- Projection: accusing you of precisely what they are doing.

- Emotional blackmail, threats, or intimidation.

- Competition – constantly compares or pits you against others or "one-up" you.

These are a few tactics narcissists can use to manipulate you into feeling bad, hurt, guilty, or ashamed. When a friend, relative, parent, teacher, manager, colleague, medical professional, or anyone else in your life constantly engages in such behavior, over time, they erode your self-worth and self-belief.

The People Who Make You Feel Guilty Are Immoral Themselves

Our moral codes of behavior dictate that we should always take responsibility for our actions. So, a person who makes others accept fault for crimes they did not commit is immoral.

People who make you feel guilty use unethical manipulation tactics, an immoral way to treat fellow human beings. Morality obliges us to treat one another as rational beings instead of mere objects and encourages us to influence each other through rational persuasion.

Furthermore, a lack of remorse for hurting others, as seen in a narcissist, is immoral since guilt and shame can be good emotions when they serve to warn us when we are wrong.

Lastly, all deliberate hurtful behavior like false accusations, abuse, comparisons, one-upping, ridicule, criticism, insults, blackmail, etc., are wrong. So, whoever participates in them can be considered immoral since knowingly hurting others is evil.

Apart from narcissists, haters are also famous for their guilt-tripping and constant destructive criticism.

It would help if you cut the haters from your life

Our society generally regards bullying or frequent exposure to haters as something people experience during childhood and puberty. For this reason, we often don't notice when fellow adults mistreat us through bullying driven by jealousy, gossip, anger, and other emotional abuse.

The truth is everyone, including good people, encounters haters, and receives hate and destructive criticism. You will always have haters regardless of who you are and the positivity you bring to the planet because nobody is immune to jealousy or hatred from others; all of us are victims of its cruelty.

A neighbor spreading false rumors concerning you, a co-worker constantly interrupting, talking over, or trying to triumph over you, or a family member making a nasty comment about you at the dinner table are all depictions of haters. Such behavior can have long-term effects if we fail to recognize and deal with them.

When I think of jealousy, the Taylor swift song *"haters gonna hate, hate, hate, hate"* comes to mind. This soundtrack handles jealous people and haters light-heartedly; by shaking them off. But, it's not always easy to shake off haters because we usually take negative comments from people we know and strangers to heart.

When hate comes from our beloved family members or close friends, we take it personally. It hurts more because their emotional expressions or actions are neither as loving nor kind as they should be. However, it would help if you understood that their jealousy usually has a root cause, which is not your fault.

So how then do you deal with;

Haters at Home

You may not chase them out of your life since they are your family. The best way to keep their negative blatant, or subtle comments away is to assert yourself and establish boundaries.

First, have an open, honest heart-to-heart about how they make you feel to show them that you are worthy of respect and appreciation the way you are. Remember to stay calm and respectful as their hurtful comments fly across rather than stoop to their indecency level. You must also clarify to the family member that their hateful behavior or comments are inappropriate and hurt your relationship.

Lastly, set boundaries if you've expressed your feelings, but the person continues with their hatefulness. It could also be wiser to limit the time you spend with that person, and if they like to tear you down using information shared in private, restrict the information you usually share about yourself and your life.

Haters at Work

If you're the target of a coworker's hate, jealousy, or negativity, it's best to confront them with the truth or ask a supervisor to intervene. It may not be easy to face someone more powerful than you or the wrong coworker, but settling issues before they worsen is best.

To limit your time with hostile workmates, ask your supervisor to assign you different projects to minimize being with them. If that's impossible, my best advice is to remain respectful and kind, be assertive, and focus on your work, ignoring their negative comments.

Online Haters

Nowadays, with the rise of social media, people can hurl insults and jabs toward those they know and strangers while hiding behind their screens. Those who feel inadequate or dissatisfied and insecure with their lives take their insults online, where you cannot confront them in person.

Delete, delete, delete!

Suppose a person comments negatively about you on your Facebook page— leverage the delete button's power— and delete the comments. If the person doesn't stop their behavior, block or unfriend them from your online platform. They will take their hate elsewhere.

Do you need a plan on how to handle your haters? Here are;

Three Strategies for Dealing With Your Haters

Sometimes, it is not possible to simply ignore or eliminate a hater because they may be people you cannot avoid entirely, like your family or coworker. That is why you need handy techniques to cope with them and ensure that even when they are around, you can still function and be happy:

Step 1: Consider The Mindset Behind The Hate

It's again about perspective. You are to pick the lens through which you perceive your haters.

Before responding to haters or deciding if you even need to respond, here are some considerations.

Is it constructive criticism or hate?

We often brand everyone who criticizes us as "haters" and dismiss them because we mostly lack the self-awareness to accept criticism, even for something we need to improve.

Of course, hostile critics are everywhere, but we sometimes adopt the phrase "haters" to avoid confronting our failures. It would be best if you realized that not everyone has mastered speaking, so some may seem slightly harsh in their remarks. Try to overlook others' semantics and focus on their statements' intentions.

Sometimes, you may get feedback you don't want to hear, whether it comes from classmates, coaches, teachers, or parents. Criticism is not necessarily "hate," it could be helpful. When someone abuses, manipulates or throws shade at you, it's unhelpful and destructive. In contrast, if what they are doing or saying is helping you, it is constructive criticism.

The big difference between these two types of criticism is their intent. If you sense that someone is intentionally trying to hurt you, be cruel to you, or tear you apart, they are critical in their approach. On the other hand, if a person is trying to point out your faults, showing you what areas you can improve, this may be constructive criticism. It may still hurt, but it's worth listening to.

Let's say your hockey teammate says, "You're a terrible skater," this is an example of destructive criticism. It's more constructive for a teammate to say, "You're a bad skater. Try bending your knees more and lower on the ice. You'll get more power in your stride."

It's not personal. Nothing is!

To live a happy life, make an effort never to take it personally. Once you understand and embody this, you'll be free from caring what others think.

Give up any desire to form opinions based on what people say or do. Try not to view their behaviors as bad or good. It has nothing to do with you and is all about them, just a background babbling of their inner struggle.

Avoid taking their criticism personally. You are on earth for an important reason. You've gotten so far by focusing on doing what you need to do—anyone who finds your outstanding performance intimidating shows you are doing something right. Don't look left or right. Stay dedicated to your path, surrounded by those who encourage you.

What kind of mental space are you responding from?

Recognize what pops up mentally, then ask yourself if the way you're reacting is by an untriggered mind or through limiting beliefs. Ask yourself when reading or hearing the comment if the following:

Your mind says you're not worthy or that what you have to say isn't good enough.

You consider switching up yourself to make others comfortable or happy.

Your instant response is to defend yourself or fight back.

All these are limiting beliefs, and you have the power to work through them.

You NEVER have to fight for your worth.

Let's be clear. NEVER question your worthiness regardless of what was said or who said it. EVER.

So what can be done to overcome these emotions and feelings?

- Be gentle with yourself and use affirmations to help you uphold your self-belief and self-love.

- Keep the focus on the bigger mission

- Stay in your lane, mentally

What NOT to do is give the negativity extra attention or any of your energy, which means don't constantly talk about it. Resist the urge to tell all of your friends and family to check out that nasty statement so you can get validated about how stupid that hater is.

Also, don't dwell on it, think about it, or let it lapse around your mind and distract you from your higher purpose. Because, in truth, that's all it's doing.

You're more powerful than a silly hate comment.

Step 2: Check In Emotionally

Before you react or respond, check in with your emotional and physical state

What's happening in your body? Check to see if:

- Your adrenaline is pumping

- Your chest feels tight
- You feel sick
- You have butterflies in your stomach

If you're feeling any of these things, PAUSE before you do anything.

If you're in fear, feeling guilty, or feeling shame, your emotions may tell you you're not safe or worthy.

Often people will want YOU to change because THEY feel bad about themselves or are triggered.

Always take your time before responding.

Have a few minutes to meditate, breathe, and physically calm yourself before you begin typing or talking.

You never know; after some time, you may realize that it's not worth it to respond!

Step 3: Action Time

Now that your mental and emotional space is in check, you can take action and weigh your choices.

Remember, before responding, assess whether the person is making a hateful comment or wants to be heard and have helpful feedback. But could work on their delivery.

Once you do that, here are some actions you can take:

Erase the comment literally or mentally. If someone has made a hateful comment for hate's sake, delete it ASAP. You don't need that in your life and don't want to subject yourself to their malevolent energy, so goodbye, hater.

Ignore the hater's comments or behavior. Responding to them even when they seem right would be trying to justify yourself to them, and you don't want to do that. Even when the conversation would be appropriate for others, it doesn't need any of your energy.

Respond to the comment. If you see an opportunity to add value to the person who said or did, or perhaps explain your intention so that they can understand it better, go ahead and respond with love, patience, and in a way that adds value to the conversation.

Here are some scenarios if you do choose to respond:

If you think someone just wants to be heard, you can say, "thank you for sharing" or "I appreciate your perspective."

If you realize someone is a back-handed hater, say, "thank you for sharing" or "you are entitled to your opinion," or ignore or delete the comment.

If you think someone has a valid point (and others like and agree with their comment), consider it and follow your heart when you give your response.

Consider forgiving your haters for raining on your parade, and excuse yourself for not carrying your umbrella.

We are not all built with equal pain tolerance, emotional maturity, and endurance. So, it's okay to show your emotions and react occasionally. You are human— calm down. And when it gets bigger, try loosening it up a bit. Understand that haters have lots of internal work to do to become a whole person due to negativity. It could be that they are also suffering, and that is what is triggering their criticism. Recognize that their negativity influences their ability to change and acquire true wisdom.

Note;

Ask yourself the following questions,

Who is in charge of your life?

Are you the pilot of your life?

Or do you feel at the mercy of forces beyond your control (like fate, gods, or another powerful force)?

Assess your "locus" of control (the degree of influence you have over your life and behavior). As psychologists suggest, it can be external or internal.

If you have an internal locus of control, you believe you're in command over your life and environment. Your successes are due to your hard work and your decisions. And you take personal responsibility for your failures and behavior.

For instance, you may say, "I passed my exams because I studied very hard." You also tend to be less obedient and less conforming (viz., more independent) and resist social pressure, perhaps because you feel in control of your actions.

But when you have an overly external locus of control, you can be inclined to rely on outside influences to shape your life and outside forces like "luck," "fate," "and chance" to determine your failures or successes. You could solely blame the actions of other people in more powerful positions and feel that there's not much you can do about it. You, therefore, say, "I passed the exam because it was easy."

Few people have an exclusively external or internal locus of control, and most of us are between the two.

Suppose your locus of control is entirely external. You may believe it's impossible to change how others perceive you (trying to do so is pointless). In that case, you may easily give up when faced with frustrations because you don't believe you have the power to change your circumstances and blame yourself for everything. Focus on inverting your locus of control when you notice it's too external.

That said...

We must always watch out for those people in our lives who like to stir up feelings of guilt and take positive action to save ourselves from them. These are only guidelines for adding to your toolbox. You can use them as handy tactics to handle both narcissistic people in your life and your haters. We must always watch out for those people in our lives who like to stir up feelings of guilt and take positive action to save ourselves from them.

Here's the thing, we're all work in progress, and if we're truly going to grow into the people who achieve the big goals we set for ourselves, it will take some shifting. The most significant thing to remember is that all this is part of the journey of self-discovery. And a big part of that is following the **Three Steps** to dealing with hater we discussed.

An essential thing in this chapter is recognizing those people in our lives who like to stir up feelings of guilt and taking positive action to save ourselves from them.

Next is an extended summary highlighting the key points to help you recap what you have learned in this book.

Conclusion

We've all had times when we clung to painful emotions like sadness, shame, and guilt for making mistakes. As transgressors, we may have profound self-doubt in our ability to solve the problem. Sometimes we don't even know how to respond to our perceived transgression(s), the responsibility we should accept for what has occurred, and whether to ask for forgiveness or not. Ultimately all we need is to engage in this soul-searching practice that leads to genuine self-forgiveness.

Self-forgiveness produces four results:

(1) The conviction that you have atoned for transgressions

(2) End of self-punishment due to mistakes that hurt others,

(3) Authentic awareness of the need for personal transformation and willingness to change behavior and feel much better about yourself

(4) It enables you to believe in yourself and others.

Self-forgiveness is a process that appreciates that the journey to healing oneself starts from within and involves navigating complex, painful, and potentially destructive emotions, including guilt, shame, fear, anger, depression, self-blame, anxiety, grief, self-hatred, or regret. Ultimately, this process leads to letting go of the self-directed painful emotions and replacing them with compassion, love, kindness, empathy, and gentleness towards oneself. By practicing self-forgiveness, you choose to live on your terms.

To recap;

Self-Forgiveness occurs in four phases.

Consider them the four therapeutic stages of self-forgiveness. As you begin your journey, find what stage you are going through and your next steps toward reaching your desired outcome.

(1) Recognition

At this point, you step back, become an observer of your behavior, and establish that you messed up. You have this silent resentment towards yourself for hurting others, making you urgently want to resolve it. You then choose self-forgiveness to release painful pent-up emotions and negative core beliefs about yourself.

It's best to employ a non-judgmental approach to examining yourself more profoundly and establish what lies behind your negative emotions through introspection. You consciously look at your mistakes to gain insight into the problem that necessitates self-forgiveness and realize how you may be unfairly blaming yourself.

After you've spent some time reflecting or picturing the event(s) and opening up unexpressed or painful feelings (like shame, hate, guilt toward yourself, etc.), you acquire self-revelation. You aim to expose the guilt and shame that consumes your soul to establish if you are using them as an alternative to cope with anxiety or other emotions or strengthen your limiting beliefs. Part of this process entails becoming aware of your inherent flaws as a human being and unlocking compassion.

(2) Responsibility

You have already identified what you said, did, or did not do that could have hurt others, and you are also ready and willing to accept responsibility for what happened. You have also evaluated your situation and sieved out the facts.

Your goal here is to re-examine what happened so that you can genuinely assume responsibility driven by understanding and empathy. Ensure that what you are forgiving yourself for is not something you are unfairly blaming yourself for, such as something you were not involved in, something you did not cause, or one beyond your control.

Use the techniques in this book to find out if the self-blame you feel could be deeply rooted in sources that might not be your fault and are hard to elude. You could be responding to a traumatic experience you did not cause - didn't ask for or want. If you discover that you suffered trauma, abuse, or loss that makes you feel ashamed and guilty even though you had no power over it, you need to identify the source, deal with it, or seek professional help.

(3) Expression

In the third stage, you actively and sincerely express the emotions revealed during self-reflection. The goal here is not to resume the usual fruitless mulling over mistakes and self-blaming but to confront and express those complicated emotions with more understanding, accountability, and compassion.

To navigate this stage of the self-forgiveness process, you may need to dialogue with yourself where you talk back to those unpleasant thoughts from a place of positivity, profound knowledge, responsibility, and empathy as covered.

It might also include a conversation with the hurt person or other people, addressing the complex feelings from a knowledgeable, compassionate point and an improved perspective.

You have learned what happened, taken your moral responsibility, and developed compassion for yourself and everyone involved. You are ultimately ready to approach others in the community or intimate people you hurt with an open heart and mind and apologize.

(4) Rebirth

The final stage of forgiving yourself is where you actively choose to recreate and redefine your self-image, make amends with the hurt person, and reconcile with yourself. During the renewal process, you freely accept the past and forge a direction for the future.

When you reach this stage, it shows you have entirely accepted everything that happened, taken justified personal responsibility, dealt with and expressed your authentic emotions to yourself and those you hurt, and learned your lessons.

Most importantly, you have also made an internal choice to forgive yourself, tell your profound regret, ask for forgiveness, try your best to repair all that went wrong, commit to changing your behavior, and live a happy life.

Remember that no situation is too tough to handle once you build trust in your intuition, applying reason and instincts to solve problems. Ultimately, you have the choice to face any problem as you wish, but what self-forgiveness does is help you build a good relationship with your inner self. You lose resentment, sadness, self-doubt, shame, blame, and guilt and gain freedom from emotional burdens as you let your mind and heart guide you toward more acceptance, lightness in spirit, compassion, and love. You stay centered on your true self and envision a positive future.

Also, remember that self-reflection is helpful, but rumination is destructive. Brooding over problems, magnifying misfortunes, and hosting a pity party escalates your distress. Consequently, whenever you rehash painful experiences, your confidence drops, hopelessness soars, and guilt intensifies.

Guilt is a helpful emotion that can signal that you have done something wrong. But, if you are not careful, it can ultimately redirect your energy to accusing, criticizing, and beating yourself up to cover past wounds or distract you from other problems. Unnecessary guilt can hinder healing, promote self-destructiveness, keep you subconsciously focused on continuing to hurt others and yourself and make you prone to many health conditions. So, dealing with and preventing it from returning is essential to self-forgiveness.

Excessive guilt does not have a magical cure. As with any strong emotion, you should consistently work on it to overcome it. To do so, you should always recognize it, reflect on it, and then let it go. You also need to weigh the source of your guilt, such as perceived wrongdoing, personality, culture, religion, level of self-awareness, toxic people, social institutions, and a poor emotional state.

Here is a summary of the steps to overcoming guilt

Understand your guilt

Recognize the function of guilt. Most of the time, we feel bad because we did or said something that hurt someone else. If it assists you in recognizing when you are at fault for something, it is both good and natural guilt. It is good because it alerts you to a mistake you made that may have harmed your relationship with someone. For example, if you neglect a friend's birthday, you may feel terrible since friends are supposed to remember and celebrate their friends' birthdays.

Recognize unproductive guilt

Before you can eliminate guilt, determine whether it is valid. Were you genuinely at fault for what happened? Is it logical to feel the way you do? Such questions may help you make sense of your guilt. Sometimes we may feel guilty when we do not need to. This type of guilt is unhealthy or unproductive because it serves no purpose. It simply makes us feel horrible.

Pay special attention to whether guilt causes you to dwell on your mistakes, preventing you from celebrating your accomplishments. For example, if you feel terrible because you had to work on your friend's birthday and could not attend her party, you are experiencing unhealthy guilt.

Your buddy should realize that you had to skip her party to keep your work. It is beyond your control if you are scheduled to work and cannot take time off for a birthday celebration. If you feel guilty about things you've not done or situations beyond your control, you need to stop it.

Here's how to quit feeling guilty when you haven't done anything wrong:

- If you decide that your guilt is unfounded, make a deliberate, active attempt to let it go.

- Avoid taking on the guilt of other people. It allows them to keep making the same mistakes and makes you suffer needlessly.

- You may need to practice dispute-resolution skills to avoid internalizing guilt that isn't yours. Try to be more forceful in disputes, stand up for yourself, and avoid apologizing when the issue does not require it.

- Choose to let go of your guilt consciously. Because the blame isn't yours to bear, keep telling yourself that there's nothing you can do but let it go.

Determine the source of your guilt.

If you feel wrong about something, you must define what you feel sorry about and why. Identifying the root of your guilt and why you feel guilty might help determine whether you have the healthy or unhealthy kind. In either case, you must go through these emotions to overcome them.

If you suffer guilt regularly, it might stem from your early experiences. Consider whether you were periodically blamed for things that went wrong, and then convince yourself that you no longer have to play that role.

Write about your feelings.

Journaling about your guilt may help you begin to understand and deal with it. Begin by writing out why you are feeling guilty. If it was something you did or said to someone, describe it as thoroughly as possible. Include in your explanation how and why this incident made you feel. Ask yourself questions. What do you believe you should be guilty of?

For instance, you may write about why you couldn't attend your friend's party. How did you react to that? What was your friend's reaction? What distracted you?

Move Past Guilt

Looking back on a situation, a moment in your life, or a conversation, you think, "Wow, I wish I had taken care of that differently. I truly messed up." To subdue the guilt, forgive yourself as you would a close friend.

Instead, say, "I made a mistake, but it doesn't make me a horrible person." When you feel guilty, take a deep breath and quit beating yourself up when you feel terrible about anything.

Sometimes it's something insignificant, and other times it's a life-changing thing. Either way, making mistakes is a part of life, but sometimes they can weigh heavily on our mental health.

They can replay like a movie repeatedly in our heads, and it can be hard to break free from. The essential thing to remember is that you are much more than your faults.

Let yourself forgive yourself and grow from the circumstances you wish you had handled better.

How can you forgive yourself when you are wrong?

To forgive oneself after hurting or wronging someone, you only need self-reflection and a willingness to change.

- Accept and confess your mistake to yourself.

- Admit that you regret your decision and wish you had done things differently.

- Think over why you committed a mistake. Were you exhausted, jealous, frustrated, furious, or anything else?

- Reflect on how you might have handled the issue better and choose to behave differently in similar circumstances in the future.

- Make apologies to those you have offended. It may not always be feasible if they are unwilling to participate; all you can do is share. Accept responsibility, provide a genuine apology, and do what is necessary.

- Be at peace with yourself. Holding on to your guilt can only worsen a bad situation. Consider the error long enough to learn from it, then move on.

Other strategies that can help you overcome your guilt alone are;

- Have an action plan for overcoming guilt

- Delete guilty perpetrators from your life, limit time spent around perpetrators, and monitor your communication with them to avoid divulging confidential stuff

- Avoid guilt-inducing information online and offline

- Understand that human is to error

- Rewire your brain, maintain positive thinking using affirmations and mantras, and counter negative thoughts with positive ones

- Tame your ego when necessary

- Observe your inner critic and correct it when negative

- Practice mindfulness every time and think about now, not the past or future

- Cultivate empathy, compassion, self-awareness, and self-acceptance

- Watch your behavior and replace bad habits with good ones

Strategies to forgive yourself with the help of others;

Sometimes people don't know what we are going through and can criticize us from the point of ignorance. To make them understand you better and help you heal from the pain of hurting yourself, use the three strategies below;

- Explain human behavior's complex aspects and how childhood conditioning influences our behavior

- Make them feel empathetic and compassionate for you

- Communicate about any traumatic experience that could be making you misbehave

To enable others to forgive you for the pain you caused when you hurt them, use the three strategies below;

- Show them that nobody is perfect and we all make mistakes

- Express that you had good intentions, which went wrong

- Explain that you never knew better when you did that to them; now you know.

After you have released your guilt through self-forgiveness, stay vigilant to ensure it never returns.

Here are some dos and don'ts for keeping guilt away.

Do

- Re-evaluate personal standards and other people's expectations of you.

- Challenge obsessive beliefs and conflicting values.

- Mind what you promise or commit to doing.

- Prioritize your life.

- Have an ongoing guilt battle plan.

- Avoid guilt-inducing things, people, and places.

- Try to forget or disconnect from bad memories using the techniques taught.

Don't

- Compare yourself to others.

- Blame yourself when things go south.

- Criticize yourself negatively.

- Use guilt for punishing yourself or others.

- As for those toxic people who inhibit us from self-forgiveness, such as haters and narcissists;

When it comes to narcissistic people, the best thing is to ignore them until they take their abuse elsewhere, but if you cannot do that, protect yourself from their manipulation using the strategies we discussed.

When it comes to haters, the first thing is to always watch out for others' intentions. Avoid instantly branding every person who criticizes you as a hater when all they could be trying to do is to help you improve at something.

If, upon scrutiny, you find that what they are saying or doing is malicious or destructive, use the strategies we learned to keep them in check. Always hold your head high and assert yourself against toxic, manipulative people to avoid looking like an easy target.

To sum it all up;

When you began the journey of forgiving and empowering yourself to let go of the past and overcome guilt, I promised three key things;

1. To help you dig deeper into your thoughts and feelings and see why you can't easily forgive yourself.

2. Teach you strategies to help you discover if it was honestly your fault or not.

3. Show you how to free yourself from the blame, anxiety, guilt, or shame you feel for wrongdoing.

From the look of things, I believe I have kept my initial promise. What is left is for you to put all you have learned into practice. Remember that self-forgiveness is not a one-day affair. It would be best if you gave it time and practice. Repetition is the mother of skill!

What is the one thing you should take away from this book?

Forgiving yourself can be tricky but doable. If you want to heal, let go of your anger, guilt, shame, grief, or any other emotion and move on, practice self-forgiveness.

It's vital to realize that forgiving oneself isn't a one-size-fits-all practice. I have given you the ideas discussed but ensure you follow your heart. Once you've identified your feelings of guilt, provide them with a voice, and remind yourself that mistakes are unavoidable.

You'll discover how liberating it can be to forgive yourself.

www.ingramcontent.com/pod-product-compliance
Lightning Source LLC
LaVergne TN
LVHW021945171224
799352LV00003B/118